VEHLMANN   JASON

ISLE OF 100,000 GRAVES

COLORING BY HUBERT

FANTAGRAPHICS BOOKS

ALSO BY JASON:

ALMOST SILENT
(collecting *The Living and the Dead, Meow, Baby!, Tell Me Something,* and *You Can't Get There From Here*)

ATHOS IN AMERICA
(Winter 2011)

HEY, WAIT...

I KILLED ADOLF HITLER

THE LAST MUSKETEER

THE LIVING AND THE DEAD

THE LEFT BANK GANG

LOW MOON

POCKET FULL OF RAIN

SSHHHH!

TELL ME SOMETHING

WEREWOLVES OF MONTPELLIER

WHAT I DID.
(Collecting *Hey, Wait...
The Iron Wagon,* and *Sshhhh!*)

WHY ARE YOU DOING THIS?

FANTAGRAPHICS BOOKS
7563 Lake City Way NE. Seattle WA 98115

Translated by Kim Thompson
Designed by Jason and Koenings
Production and lettering by Paul Baresh
Associate Publisher: Eric Reynolds
Published by Gary Groth and Kim Thompson

Special thanks to Etienne Bonnin
at Editions Glénat.

To receive a free catalog of comics, call 1-800-657-1100 or
write us at Fantagraphics Books, 7563 Lake City Way NE,
Seattle, WA 98115.

Distributed in the U.S. by W.W. Norton and Company, Inc.
(800-233-4830)
Distributed in Canada by Canadian Manda Group
(fax 888-563-8327)
Distributed in the United Kingdom by Turnaround
Distribution (44 (0)20 8829-3002)
Distributed to the comics market by Diamond Comic
Distributors, Inc. (800-452-6642 x215)

Visit the website for The Beguiling, where Jason's original
artwork can be purchased: www.beguiling.com
Visit the Fantagraphics website: www.fantagraphics.com

First printing: May, 2011

ISBN: 978-1-60699-442-9

Printed in China

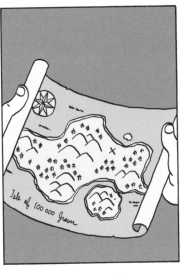

Isle of 100 000 Graves

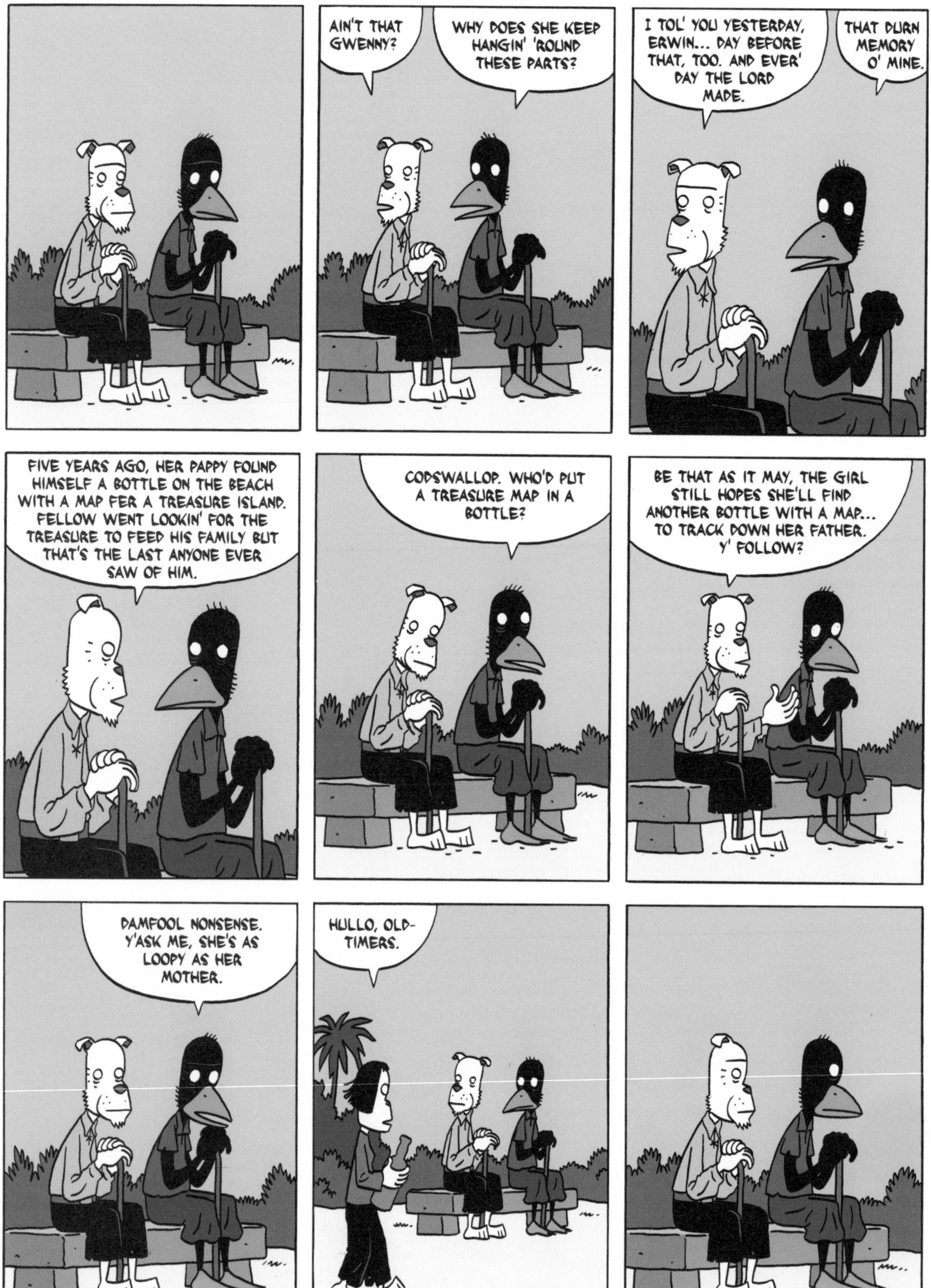
AIN'T THAT GWENNY?
WHY DOES SHE KEEP HANGIN' 'ROUND THESE PARTS?
I TOL' YOU YESTERDAY, ERWIN... DAY BEFORE THAT, TOO. AND EVER' DAY THE LORD MADE.
THAT DURN MEMORY O' MINE.
FIVE YEARS AGO, HER PAPPY FOUND HIMSELF A BOTTLE ON THE BEACH WITH A MAP FER A TREASURE ISLAND. FELLOW WENT LOOKIN' FOR THE TREASURE TO FEED HIS FAMILY BUT THAT'S THE LAST ANYONE EVER SAW OF HIM.
CODSWALLOP. WHO'D PUT A TREASURE MAP IN A BOTTLE?
BE THAT AS IT MAY, THE GIRL STILL HOPES SHE'LL FIND ANOTHER BOTTLE WITH A MAP... TO TRACK DOWN HER FATHER. Y' FOLLOW?
DAMFOOL NONSENSE. Y'ASK ME, SHE'S AS LOOPY AS HER MOTHER.
HULLO, OLD-TIMERS.

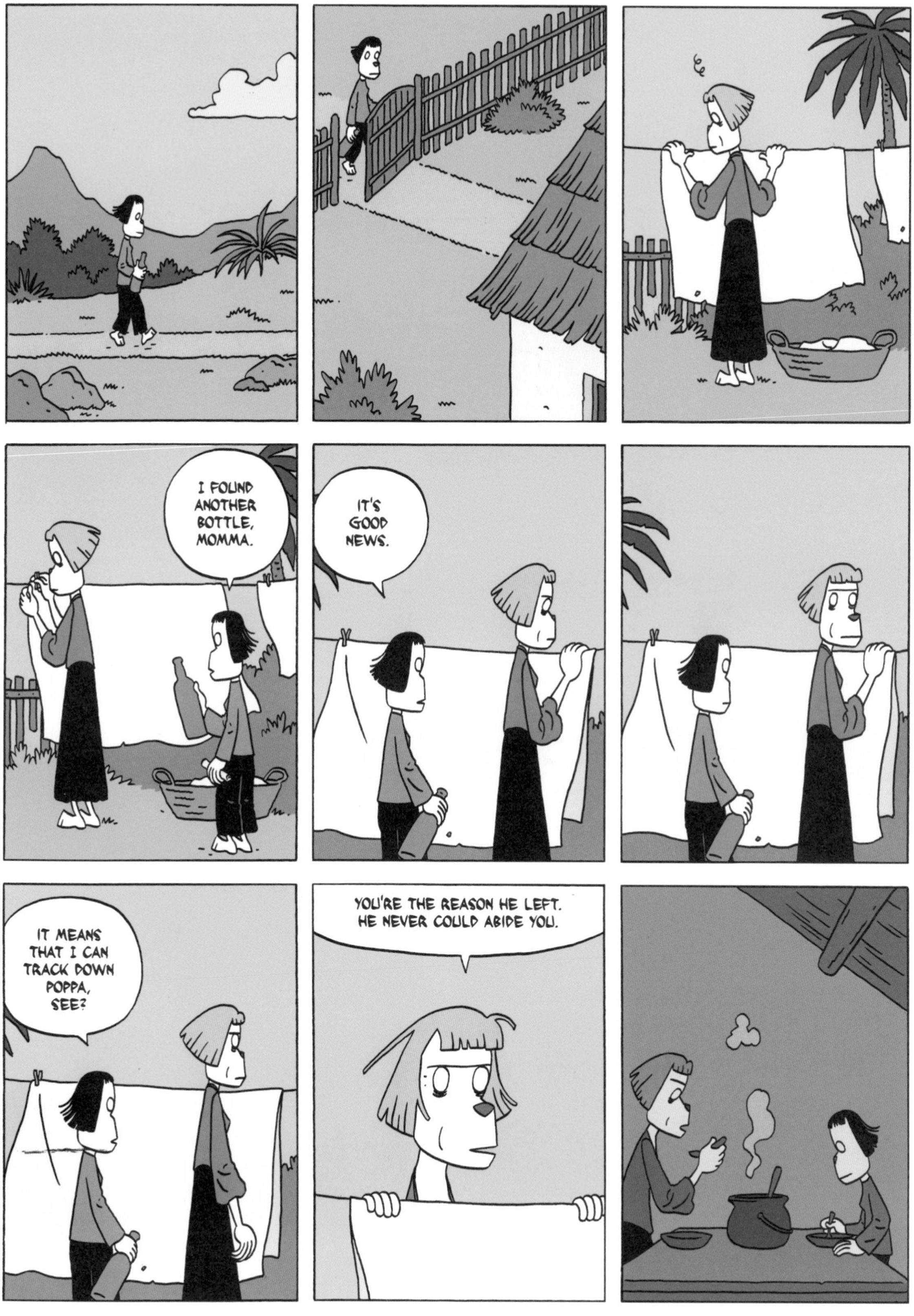
I FOUND ANOTHER BOTTLE, MOMMA.
IT'S GOOD NEWS.
IT MEANS THAT I CAN TRACK DOWN POPPA, SEE?
YOU'RE THE REASON HE LEFT. HE NEVER COULD ABIDE YOU.

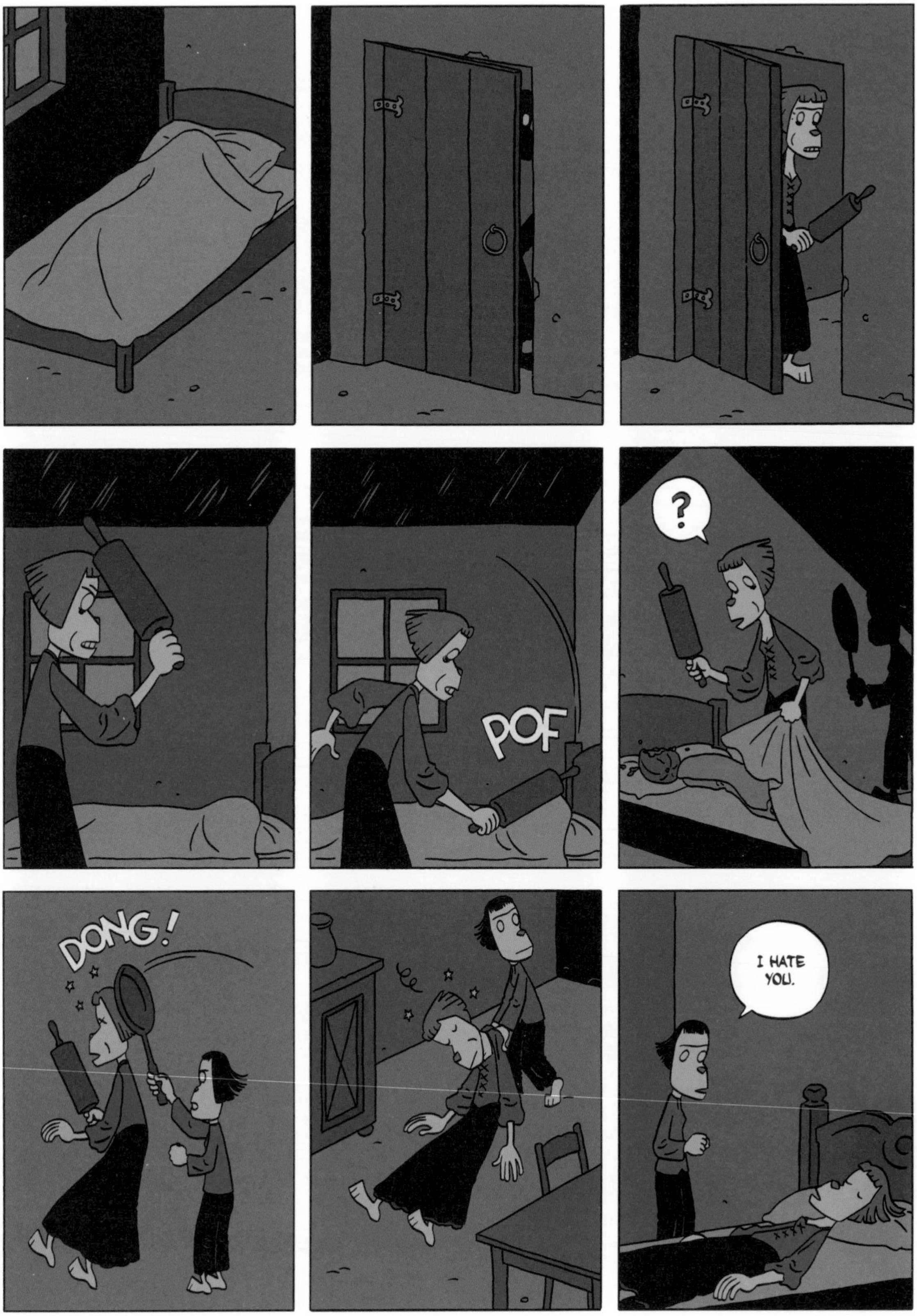
POF
?
DONG!
I HATE YOU.

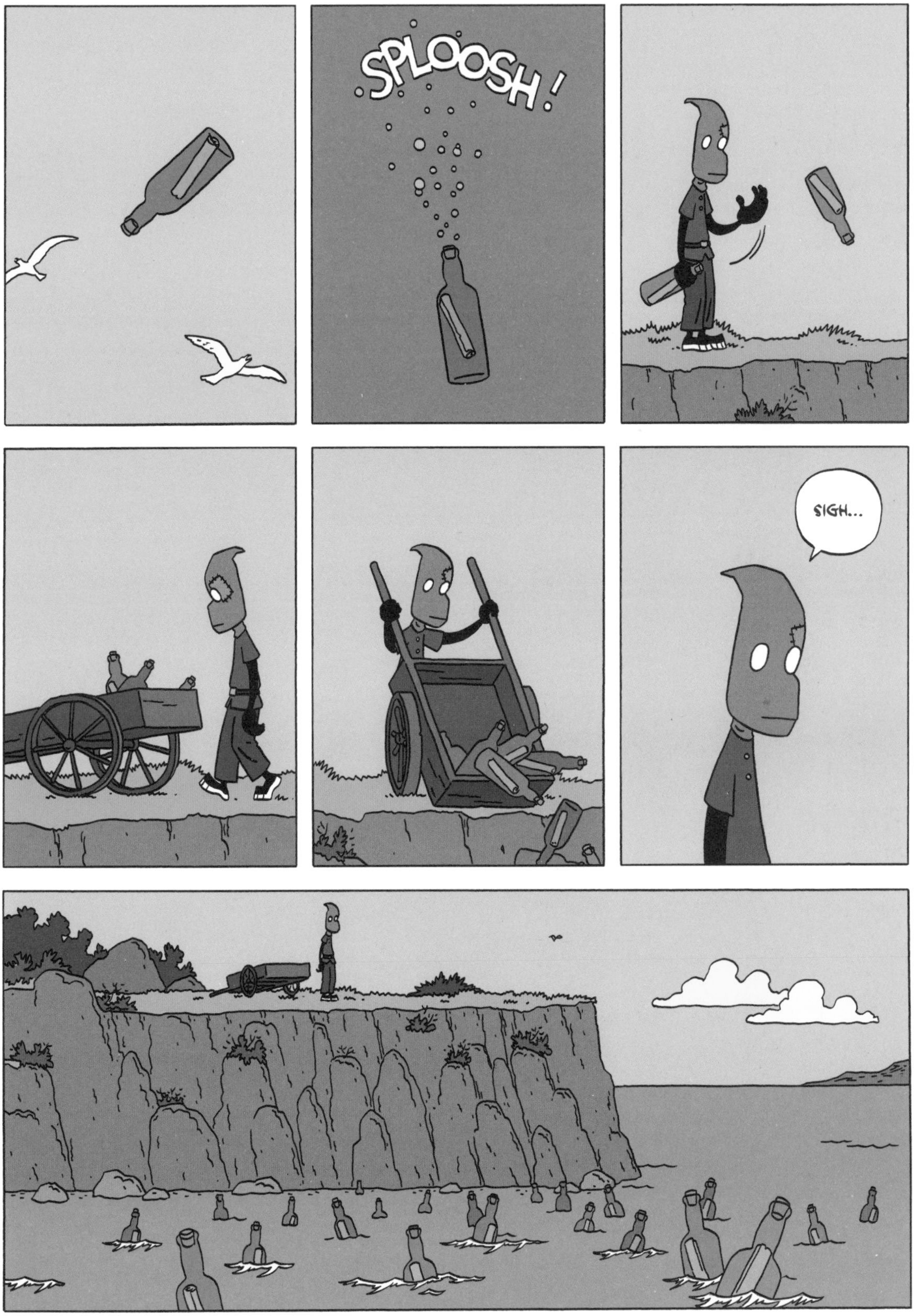
SPLOOSH!
SIGH...

I NEED ME SOME SAILORS TO FIND A TREASURE.
GET LOST.
IT'S THE TREASURE OF THE ISLE OF 100,000 GRAVES.
THE LEGENDARY TREA-SURE...
THE ISLE OF 100,000 GRAVES. MANY HAVE SOUGHT IT BUT NONE HAS EVER RETURNED.
I FOUND A MAP THAT SHOWS WHERE THE ISLAND IS. I'LL GUIDE YOU IF YOU TAKE ME WITH YOU.
HAVE YOU GOT THIS MAP ON YOU?
NO. I ATE IT.
HOW LONG AGO?
COUPLE OF DAYS.
OH, WELL.

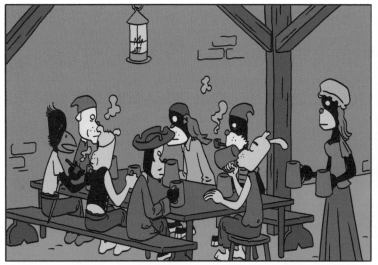

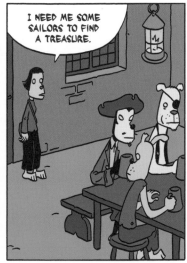

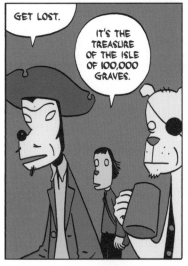

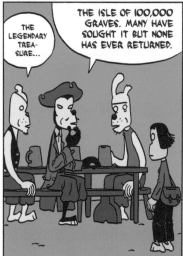

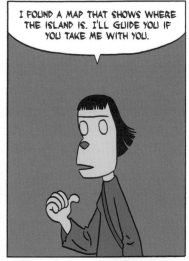

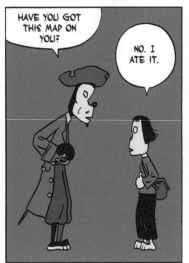

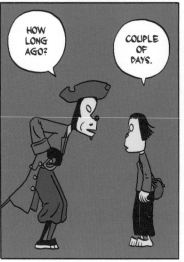

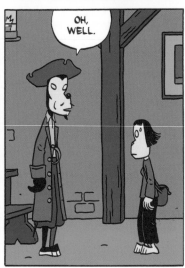

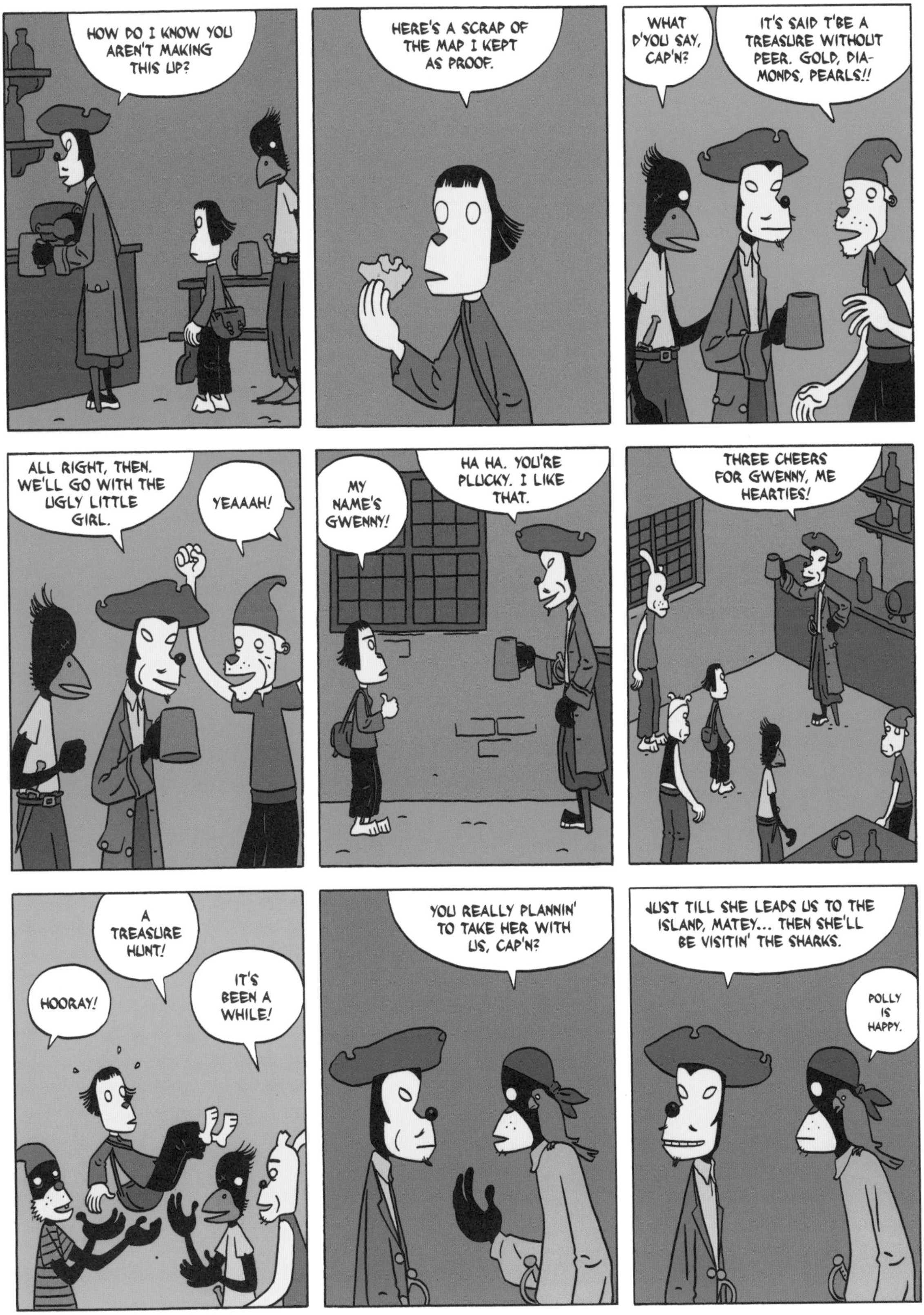
HOW DO I KNOW YOU AREN'T MAKING THIS UP?
HERE'S A SCRAP OF THE MAP I KEPT AS PROOF.
WHAT D'YOU SAY, CAP'N?
IT'S SAID T'BE A TREASURE WITHOUT PEER. GOLD, DIA-MONDS, PEARLS!!
ALL RIGHT, THEN. WE'LL GO WITH THE UGLY LITTLE GIRL.
YEAAAH!
MY NAME'S GWENNY!
HA HA. YOU'RE PLUCKY. I LIKE THAT.
THREE CHEERS FOR GWENNY, ME HEARTIES!
A TREASURE HUNT!
HOORAY!
IT'S BEEN A WHILE!
YOU REALLY PLANNIN' TO TAKE HER WITH US, CAP'N?
JUST TILL SHE LEADS US TO THE ISLAND, MATEY... THEN SHE'LL BE VISITIN' THE SHARKS.
POLLY IS HAPPY.

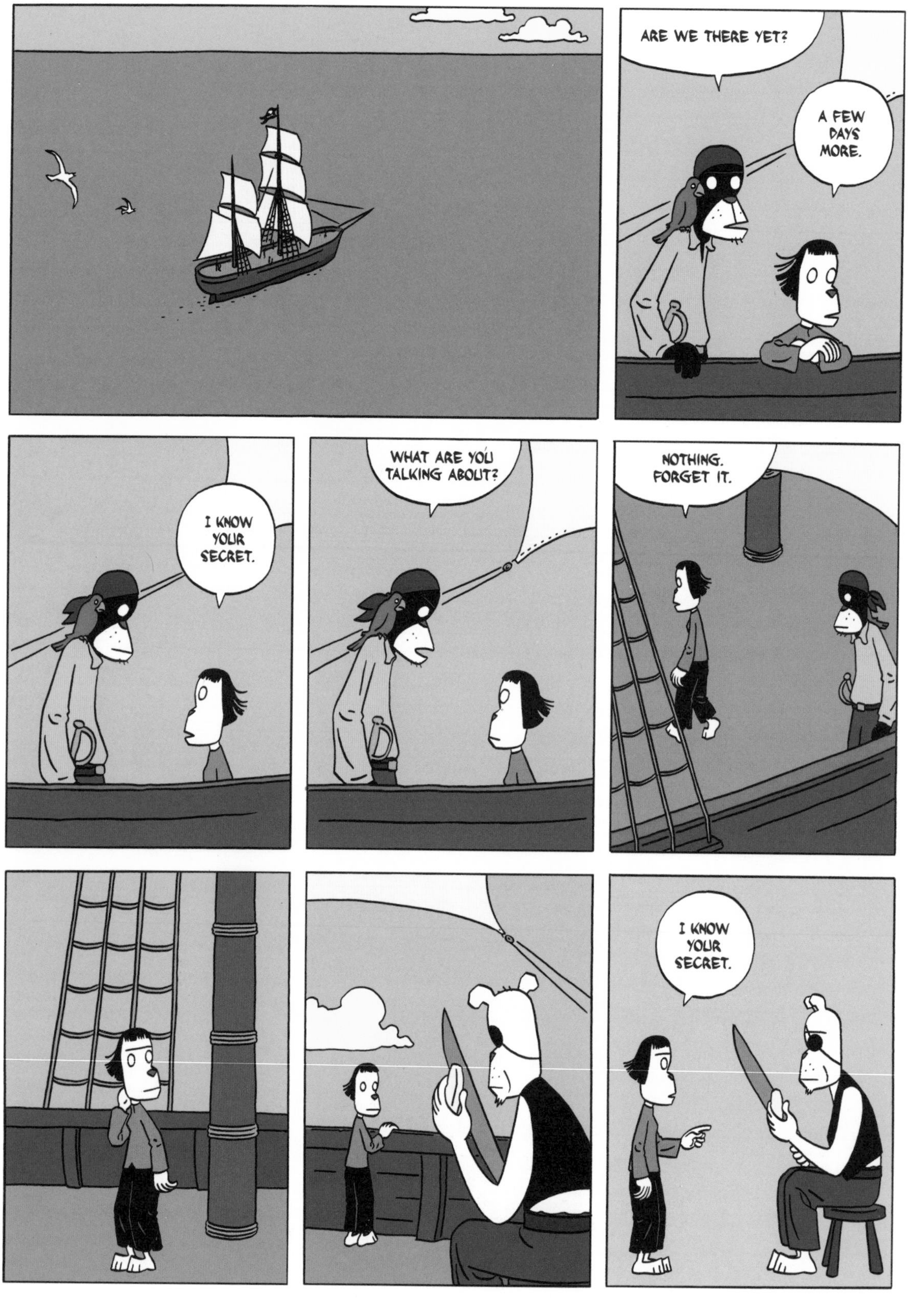
ARE WE THERE YET?
A FEW DAYS MORE.
I KNOW YOUR SECRET.
WHAT ARE YOU TALKING ABOUT?
NOTHING. FORGET IT.
I KNOW YOUR SECRET.

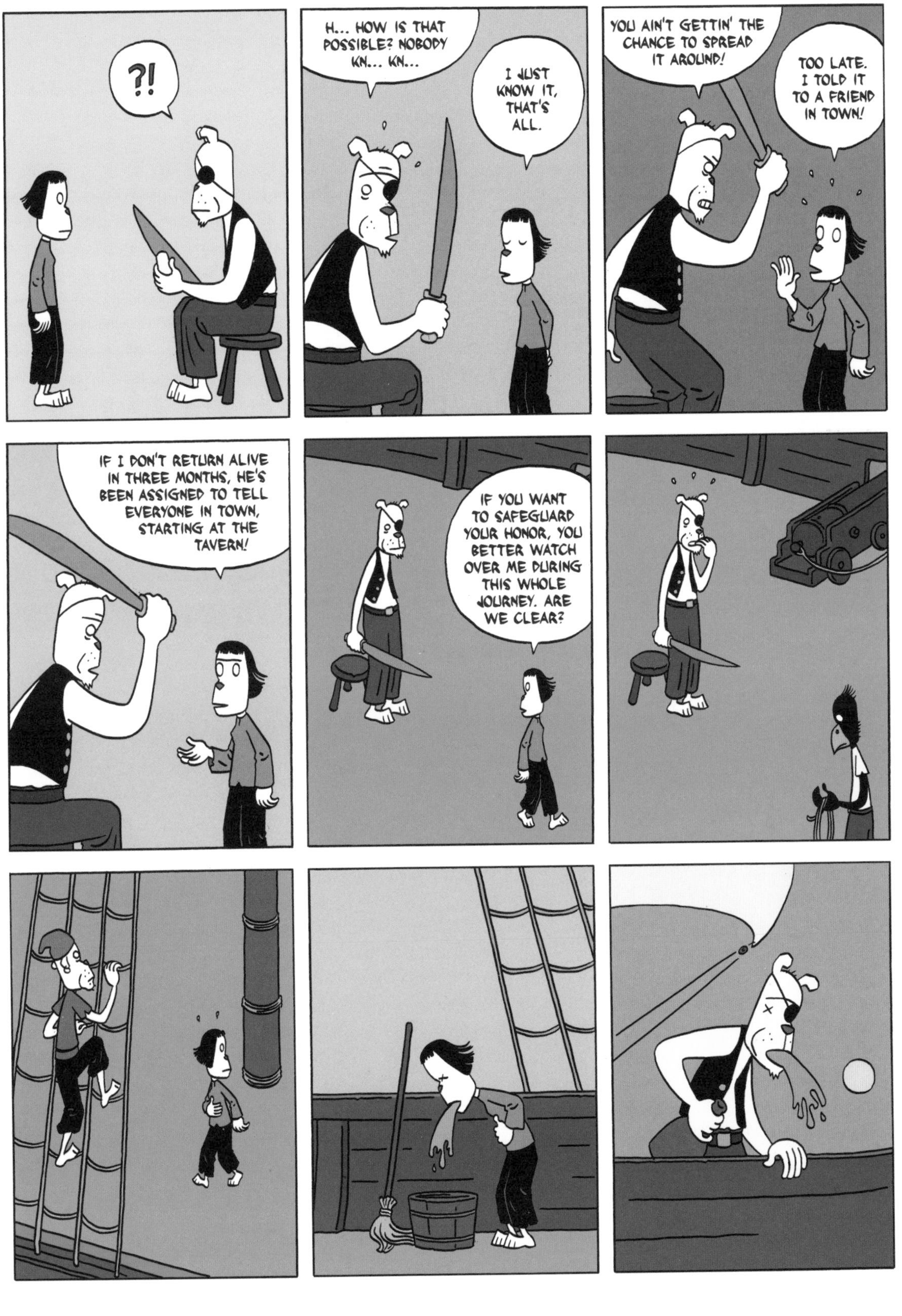
?!
H... HOW IS THAT POSSIBLE? NOBODY KN... KN...
I JUST KNOW IT, THAT'S ALL.
YOU AIN'T GETTIN' THE CHANCE TO SPREAD IT AROUND!
TOO LATE. I TOLD IT TO A FRIEND IN TOWN!
IF I DON'T RETURN ALIVE IN THREE MONTHS, HE'S BEEN ASSIGNED TO TELL EVERYONE IN TOWN, STARTING AT THE TAVERN!
IF YOU WANT TO SAFEGUARD YOUR HONOR, YOU BETTER WATCH OVER ME DURING THIS WHOLE JOURNEY. ARE WE CLEAR?

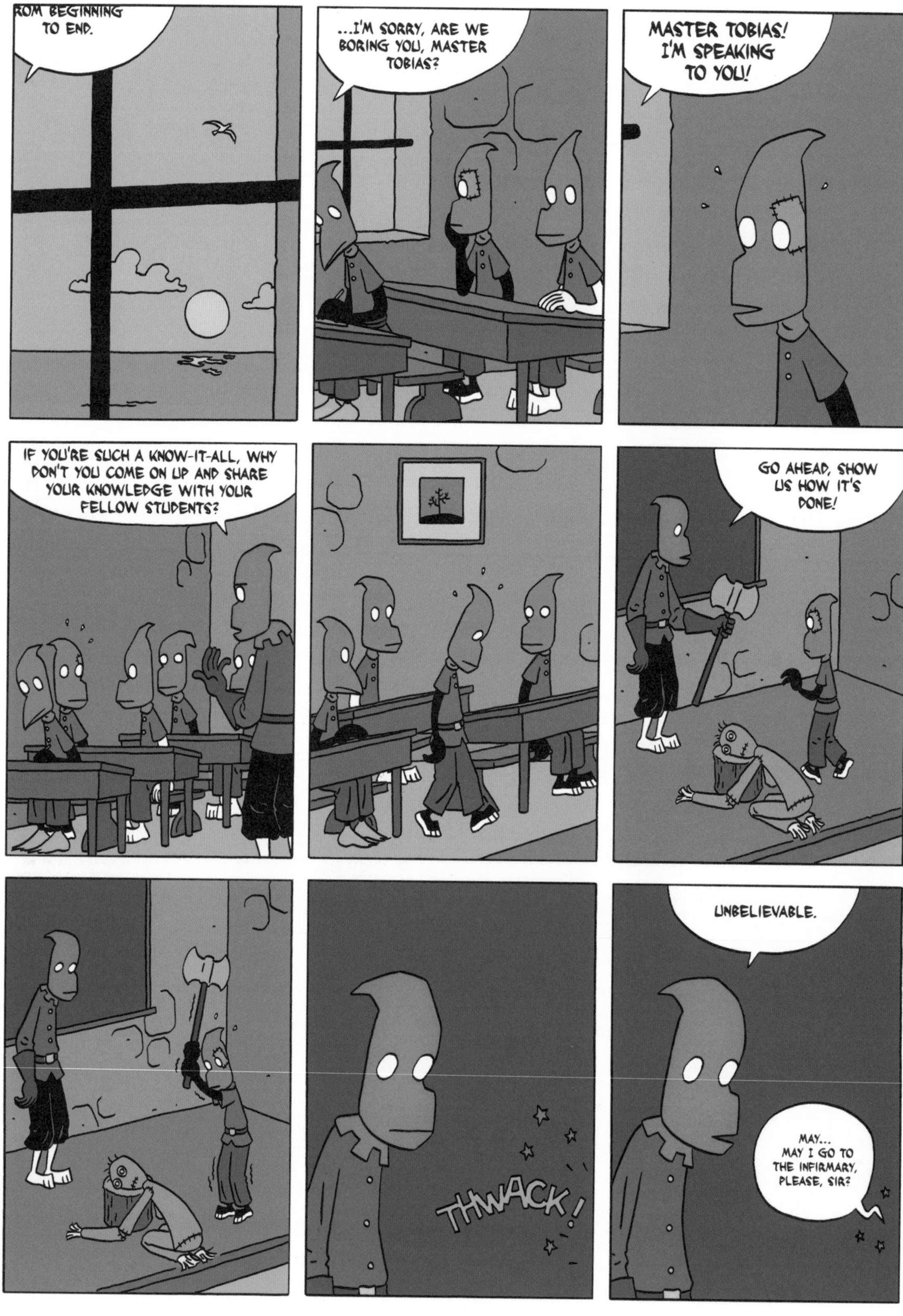
ROM BEGINNING TO END.
...I'M SORRY, ARE WE BORING YOU, MASTER TOBIAS?
MASTER TOBIAS! I'M SPEAKING TO YOU!
IF YOU'RE SUCH A KNOW-IT-ALL, WHY DON'T YOU COME ON UP AND SHARE YOUR KNOWLEDGE WITH YOUR FELLOW STUDENTS?
GO AHEAD, SHOW US HOW IT'S DONE!
THWACK!
UNBELIEVABLE.
MAY... MAY I GO TO THE INFIRMARY, PLEASE, SIR?

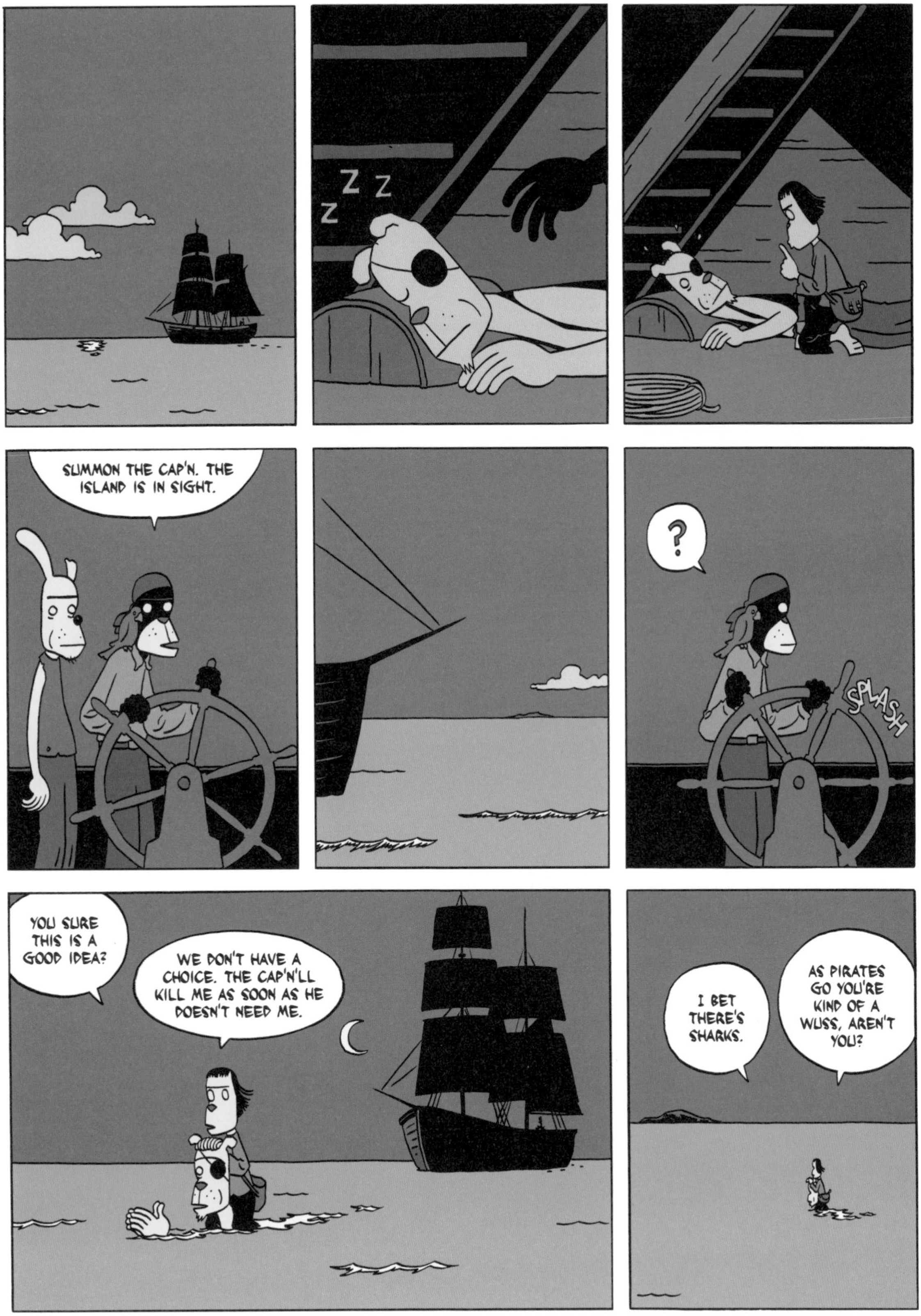
Z Z Z
SUMMON THE CAP'N. THE ISLAND IS IN SIGHT.
?
SPLASH
YOU SURE THIS IS A GOOD IDEA?
WE DON'T HAVE A CHOICE. THE CAP'N'LL KILL ME AS SOON AS HE DOESN'T NEED ME.
I BET THERE'S SHARKS.
AS PIRATES GO YOU'RE KIND OF A WUSS, AREN'T YOU?

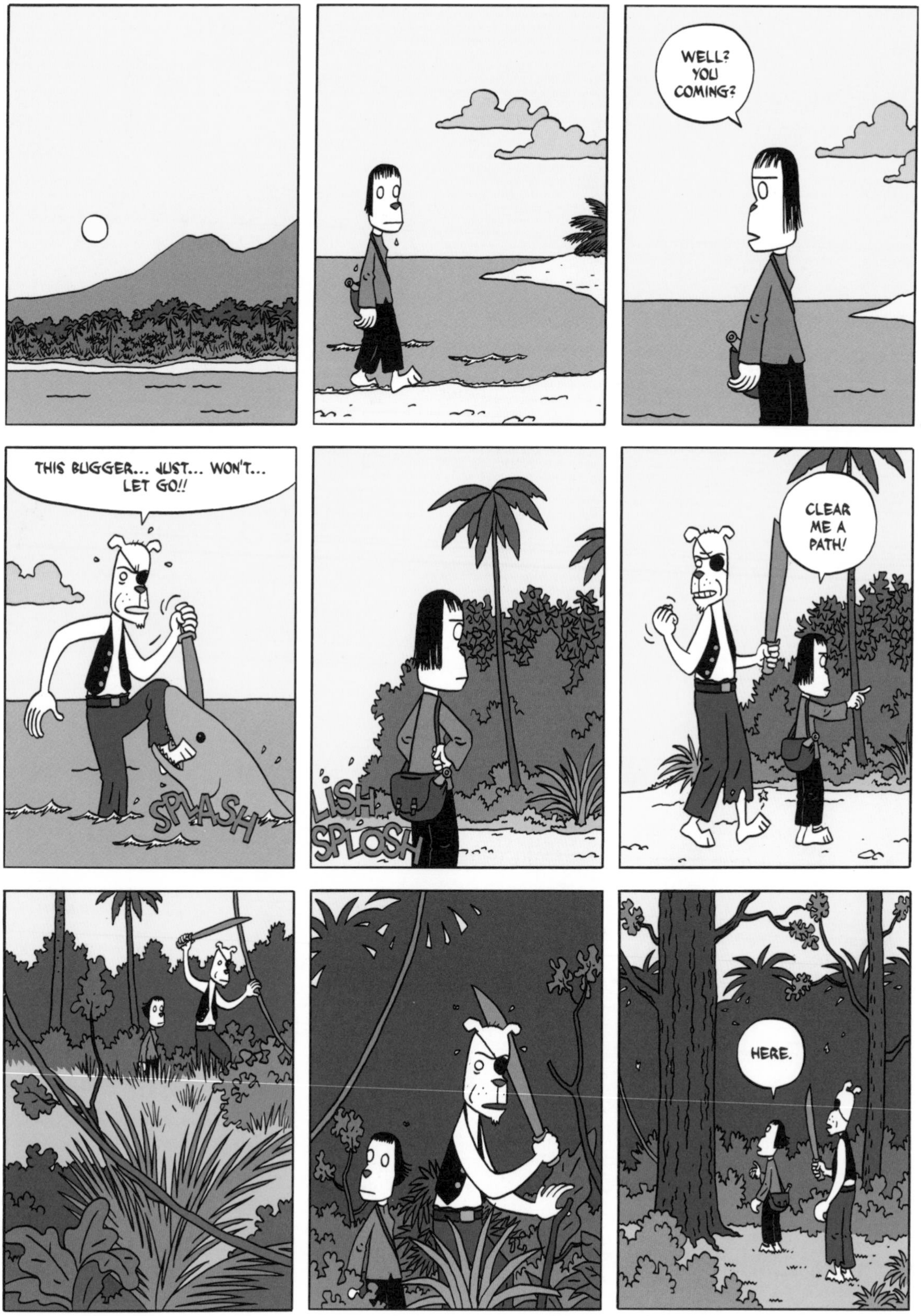

WELL? YOU COMING?
THIS BUGGER... JUST... WON'T... LET GO!!
SPLASH
LISH SPLOSH
CLEAR ME A PATH!
HERE.

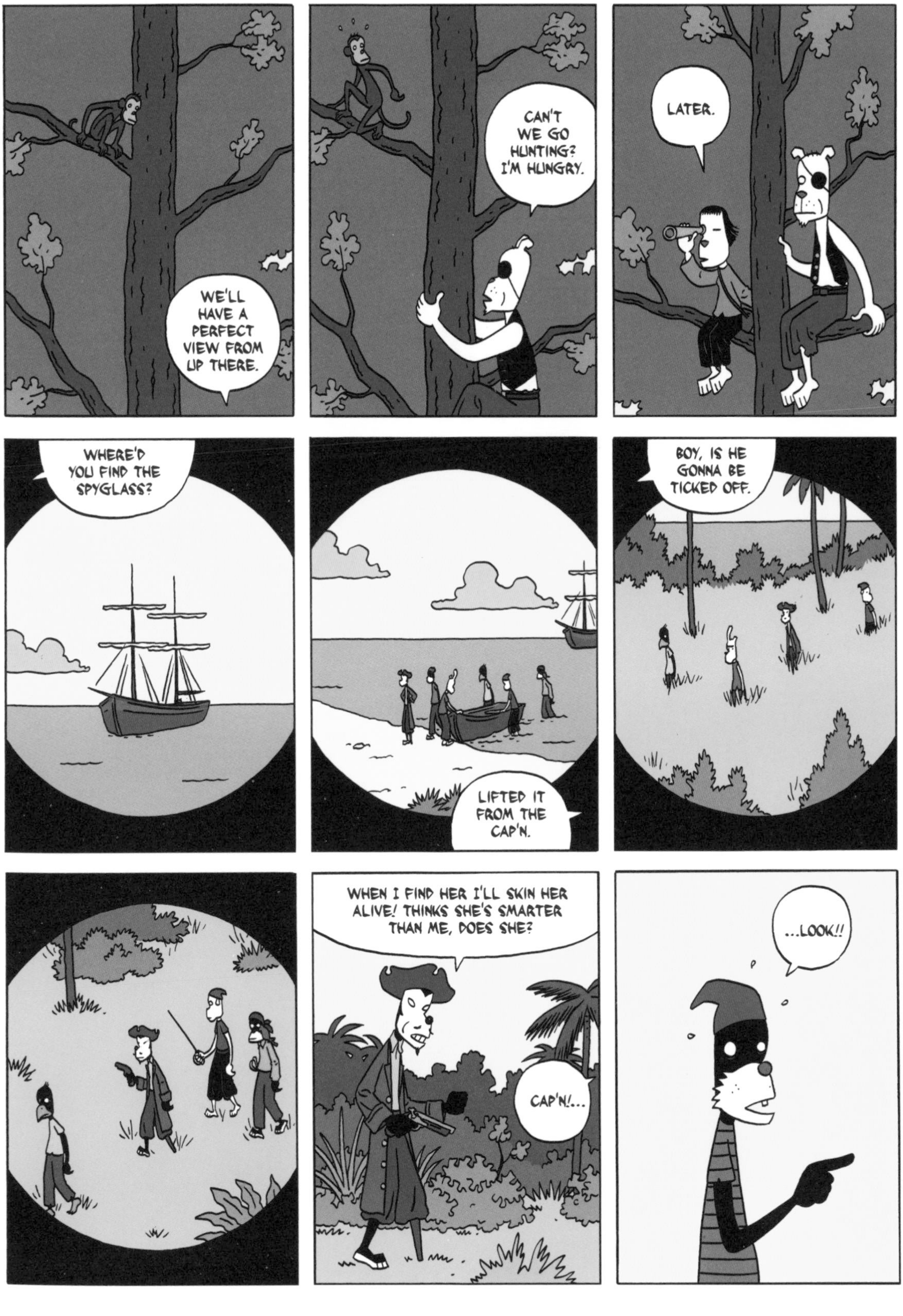
WE'LL HAVE A PERFECT VIEW FROM UP THERE.
CAN'T WE GO HUNTING? I'M HUNGRY.
LATER.
WHERE'D YOU FIND THE SPYGLASS?
LIFTED IT FROM THE CAP'N.
BOY, IS HE GONNA BE TICKED OFF.
WHEN I FIND HER I'LL SKIN HER ALIVE! THINKS SHE'S SMARTER THAN ME, DOES SHE?
CAP'N!...
...LOOK!!

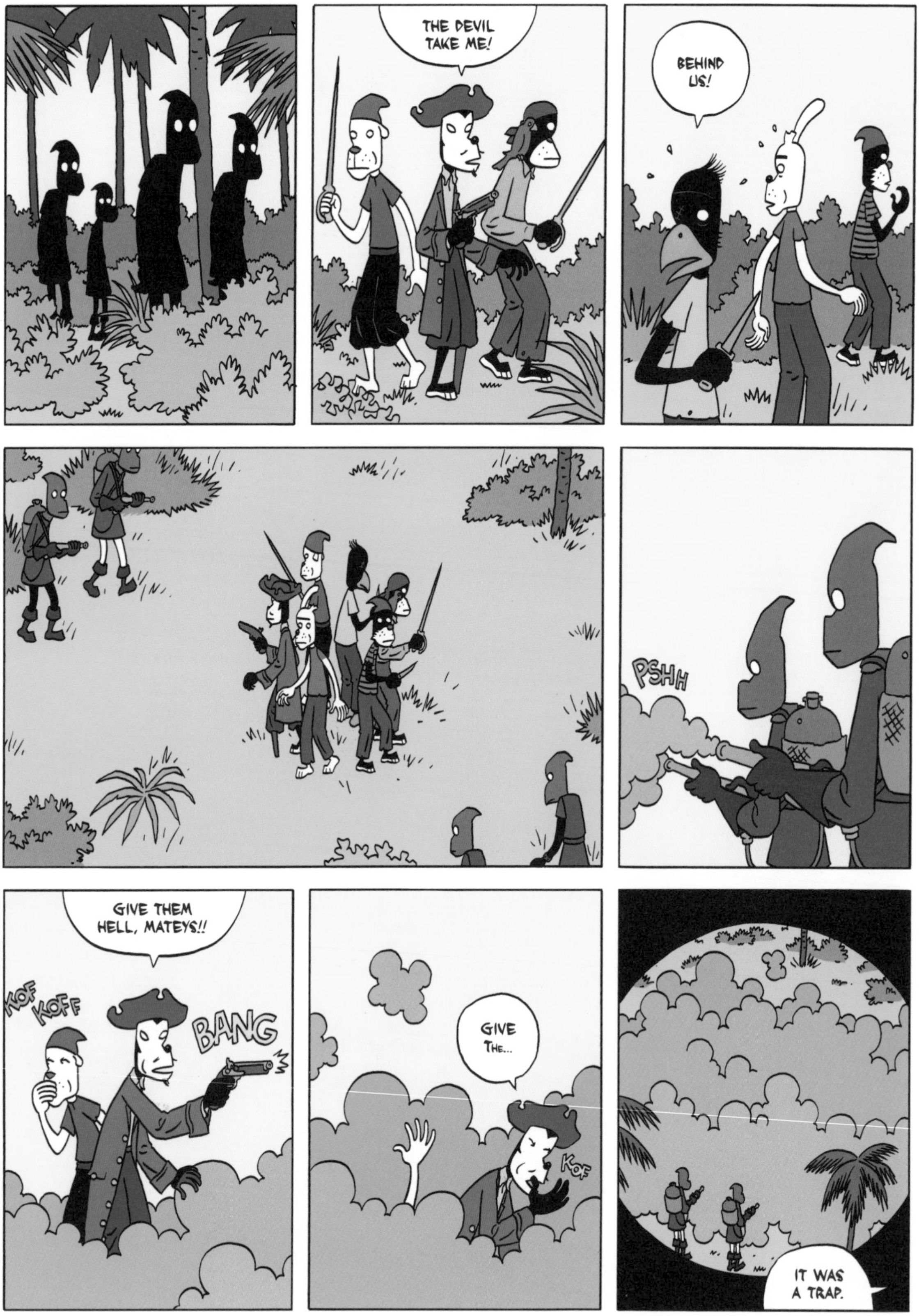
THE DEVIL TAKE ME!
BEHIND US!
PSHH
GIVE THEM HELL, MATEYS!!
KOF KOFF
BANG
GIVE THE...
KOF
IT WAS A TRAP.

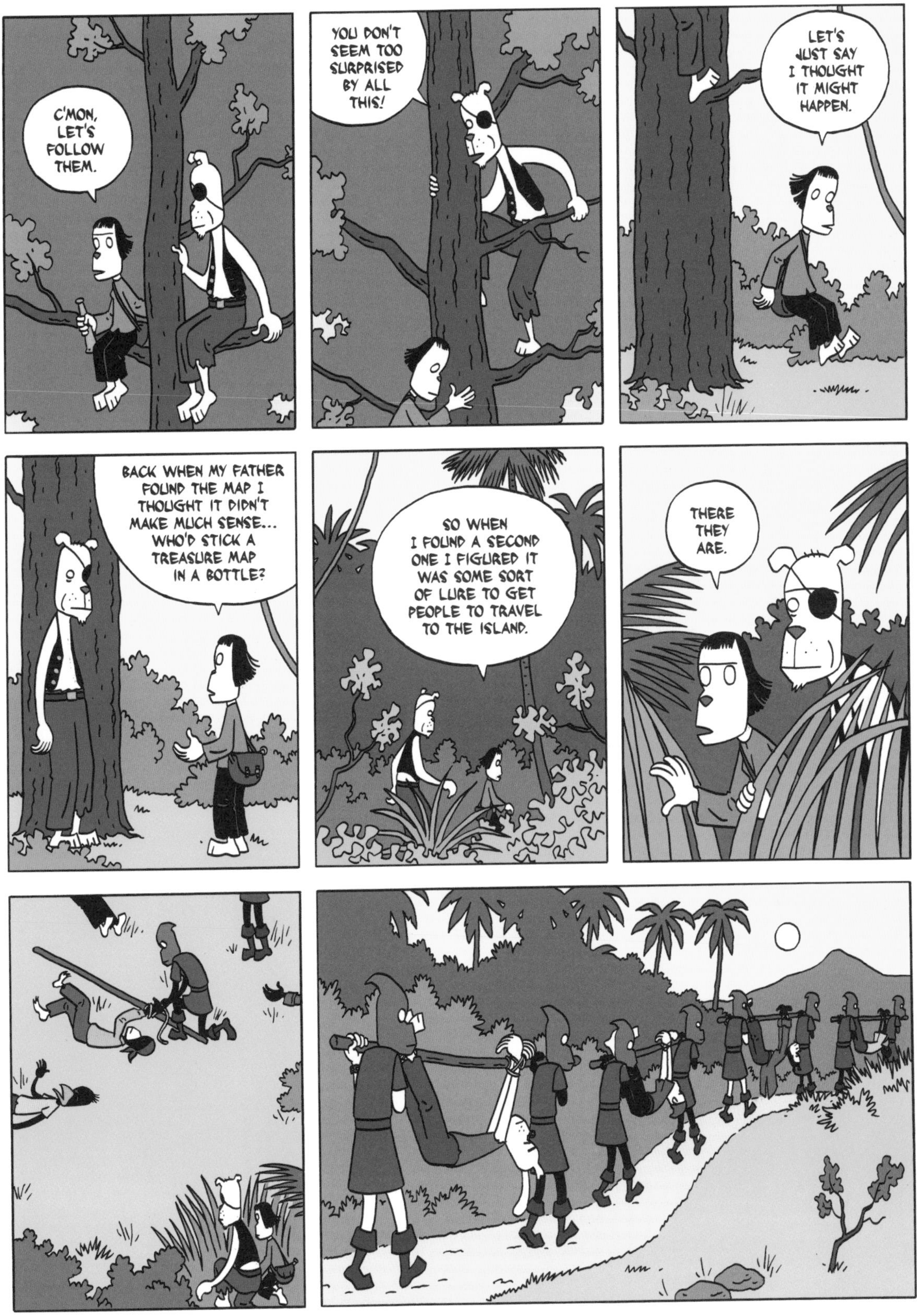
C'MON, LET'S FOLLOW THEM.
YOU DON'T SEEM TOO SURPRISED BY ALL THIS!
LET'S JUST SAY I THOUGHT IT MIGHT HAPPEN.
BACK WHEN MY FATHER FOUND THE MAP I THOUGHT IT DIDN'T MAKE MUCH SENSE... WHO'D STICK A TREASURE MAP IN A BOTTLE?
SO WHEN I FOUND A SECOND ONE I FIGURED IT WAS SOME SORT OF LURE TO GET PEOPLE TO TRAVEL TO THE ISLAND.
THERE THEY ARE.

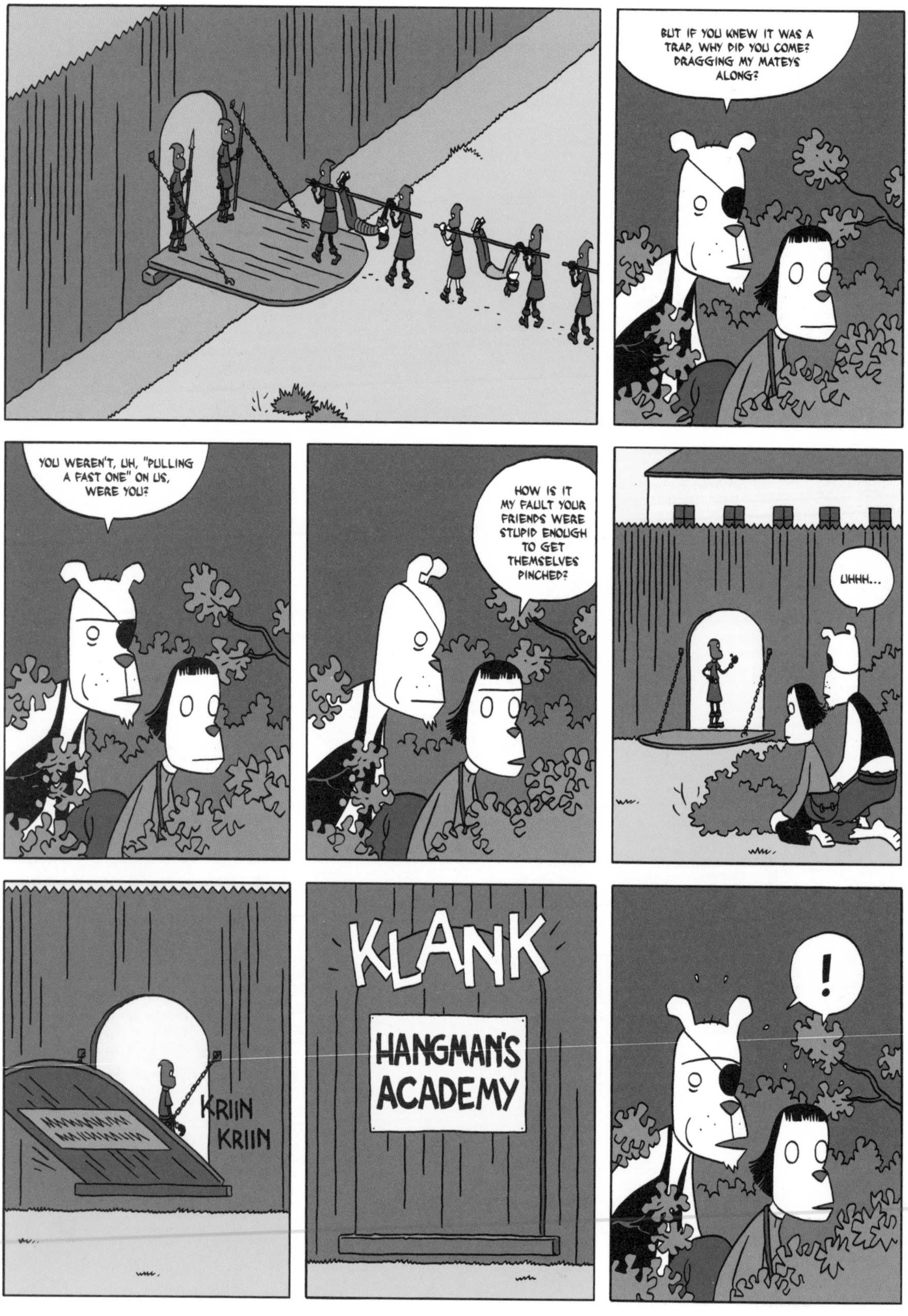

BUT IF YOU KNEW IT WAS A TRAP, WHY DID YOU COME? DRAGGING MY MATEYS ALONG?
YOU WEREN'T, UH, "PULLING A FAST ONE" ON US, WERE YOU?
HOW IS IT MY FAULT YOUR FRIENDS WERE STUPID ENOUGH TO GET THEMSELVES PINCHED?
UHHH...
KRIIN
KRIIN
KLANK
HANGMAN'S ACADEMY
!

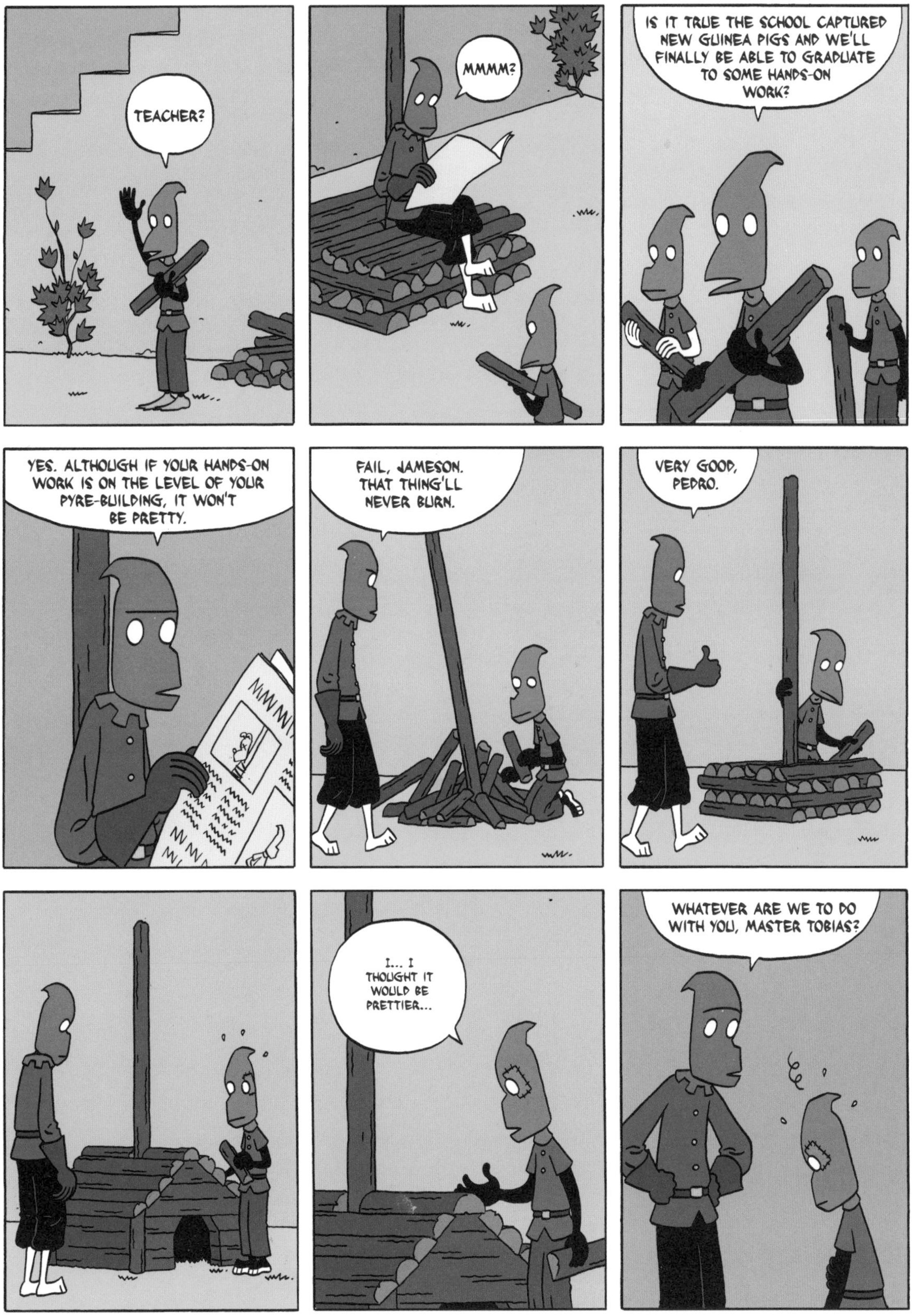
TEACHER?
MMMM?
IS IT TRUE THE SCHOOL CAPTURED NEW GUINEA PIGS AND WE'LL FINALLY BE ABLE TO GRADUATE TO SOME HANDS-ON WORK?
YES. ALTHOUGH IF YOUR HANDS-ON WORK IS ON THE LEVEL OF YOUR PYRE-BUILDING, IT WON'T BE PRETTY.
FAIL, JAMESON. THAT THING'LL NEVER BURN.
VERY GOOD, PEDRO.
I... I THOUGHT IT WOULD BE PRETTIER...
WHATEVER ARE WE TO DO WITH YOU, MASTER TOBIAS?

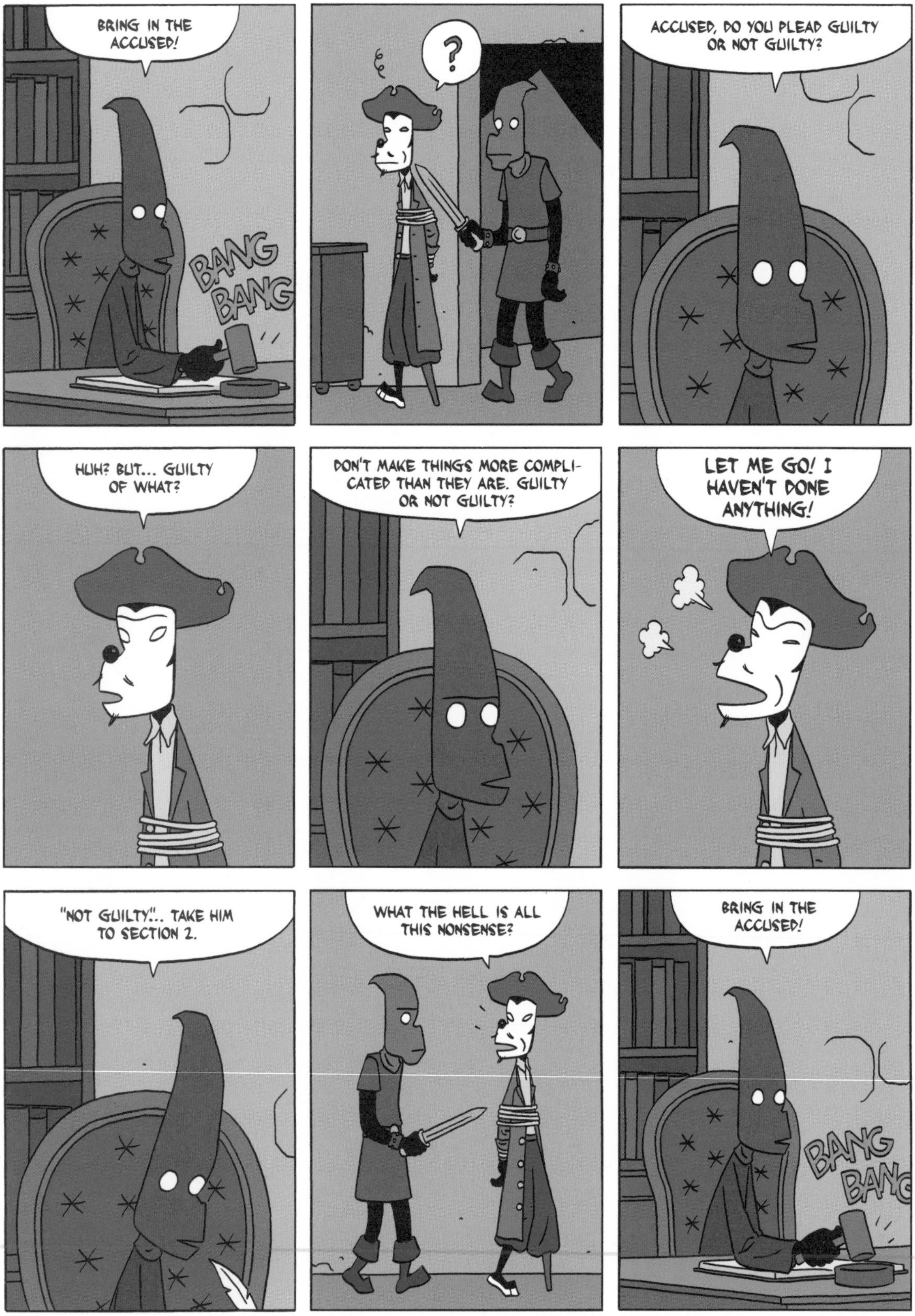
BRING IN THE ACCUSED!
BANG BANG
?
ACCUSED, DO YOU PLEAD GUILTY OR NOT GUILTY?
HUH? BUT... GUILTY OF WHAT?
DON'T MAKE THINGS MORE COMPLICATED THAN THEY ARE. GUILTY OR NOT GUILTY?
LET ME GO! I HAVEN'T DONE ANYTHING!
"NOT GUILTY!"... TAKE HIM TO SECTION 2.
WHAT THE HELL IS ALL THIS NONSENSE?
BRING IN THE ACCUSED!
BANG BANG

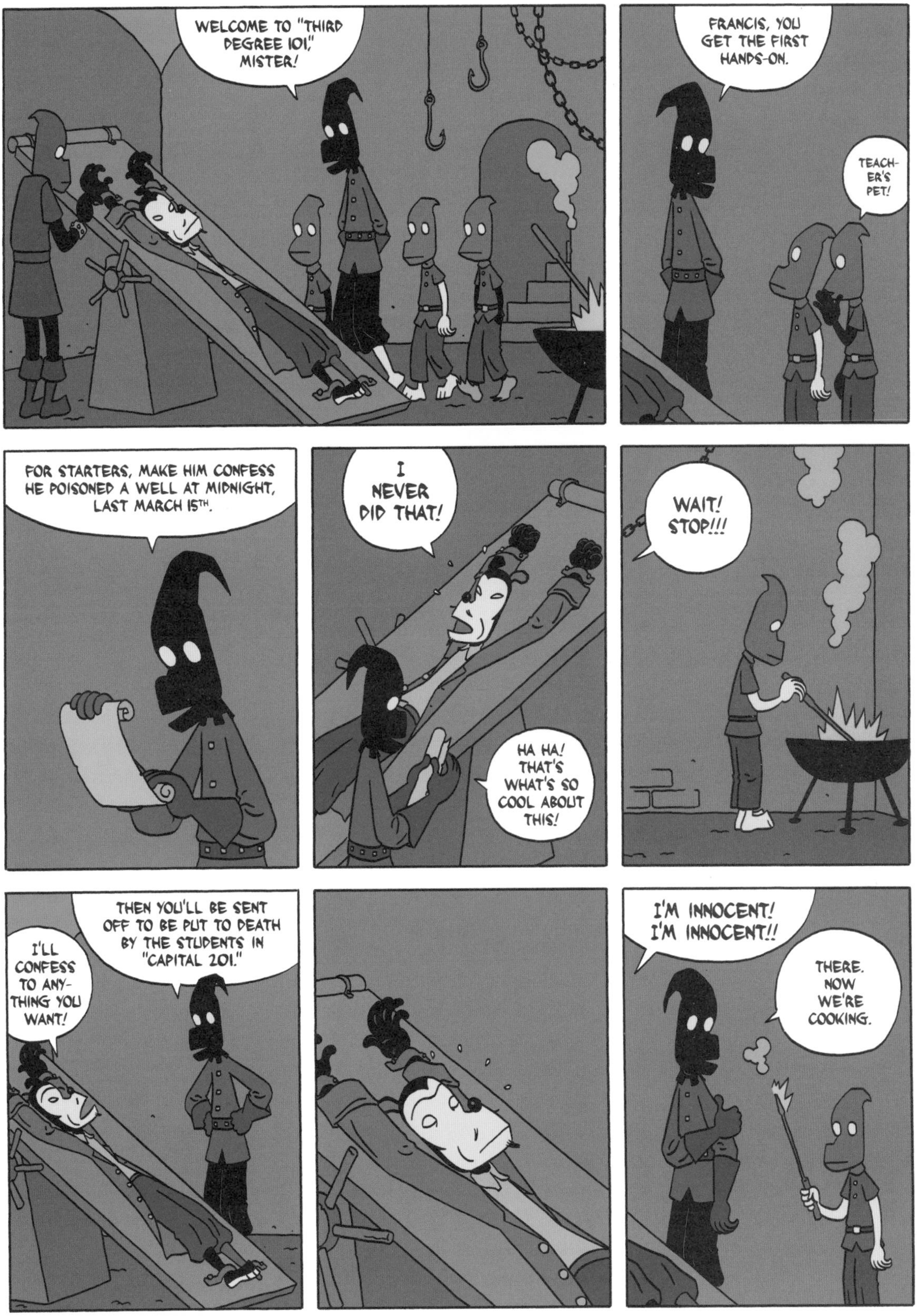
WELCOME TO "THIRD DEGREE 101," MISTER!
FRANCIS, YOU GET THE FIRST HANDS-ON.
TEACH-ER'S PET!
FOR STARTERS, MAKE HIM CONFESS HE POISONED A WELL AT MIDNIGHT, LAST MARCH 15TH.
I NEVER DID THAT!
HA HA! THAT'S WHAT'S SO COOL ABOUT THIS!
WAIT! STOP!!!
I'LL CONFESS TO ANY-THING YOU WANT!
THEN YOU'LL BE SENT OFF TO BE PUT TO DEATH BY THE STUDENTS IN "CAPITAL 201."
I'M INNOCENT! I'M INNOCENT!!
THERE. NOW WE'RE COOKING.

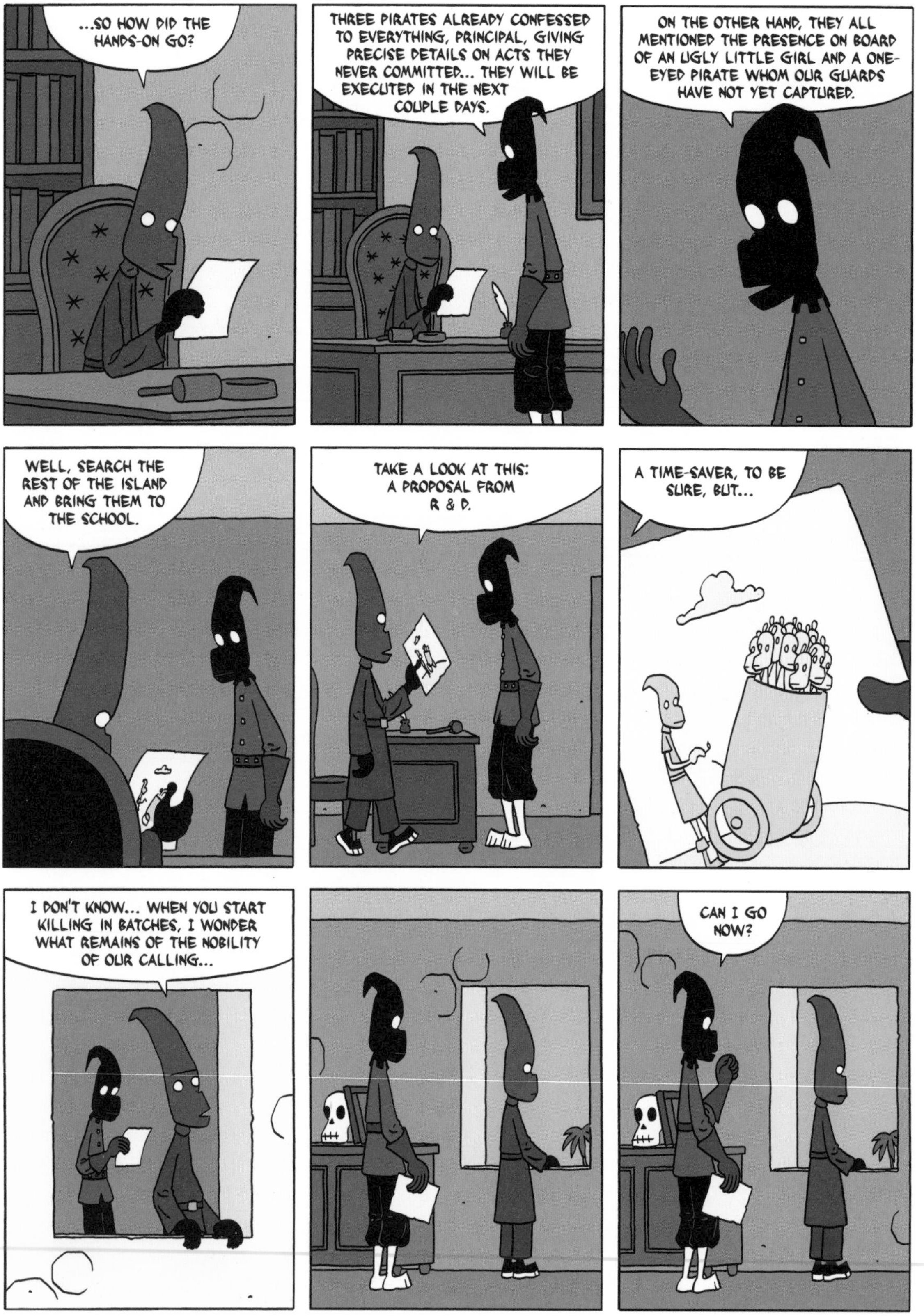
...SO HOW DID THE HANDS-ON GO?
THREE PIRATES ALREADY CONFESSED TO EVERYTHING, PRINCIPAL, GIVING PRECISE DETAILS ON ACTS THEY NEVER COMMITTED... THEY WILL BE EXECUTED IN THE NEXT COUPLE DAYS.
ON THE OTHER HAND, THEY ALL MENTIONED THE PRESENCE ON BOARD OF AN UGLY LITTLE GIRL AND A ONE-EYED PIRATE WHOM OUR GUARDS HAVE NOT YET CAPTURED.
WELL, SEARCH THE REST OF THE ISLAND AND BRING THEM TO THE SCHOOL.
TAKE A LOOK AT THIS: A PROPOSAL FROM R & D.
A TIME-SAVER, TO BE SURE, BUT...
I DON'T KNOW... WHEN YOU START KILLING IN BATCHES, I WONDER WHAT REMAINS OF THE NOBILITY OF OUR CALLING...
CAN I GO NOW?

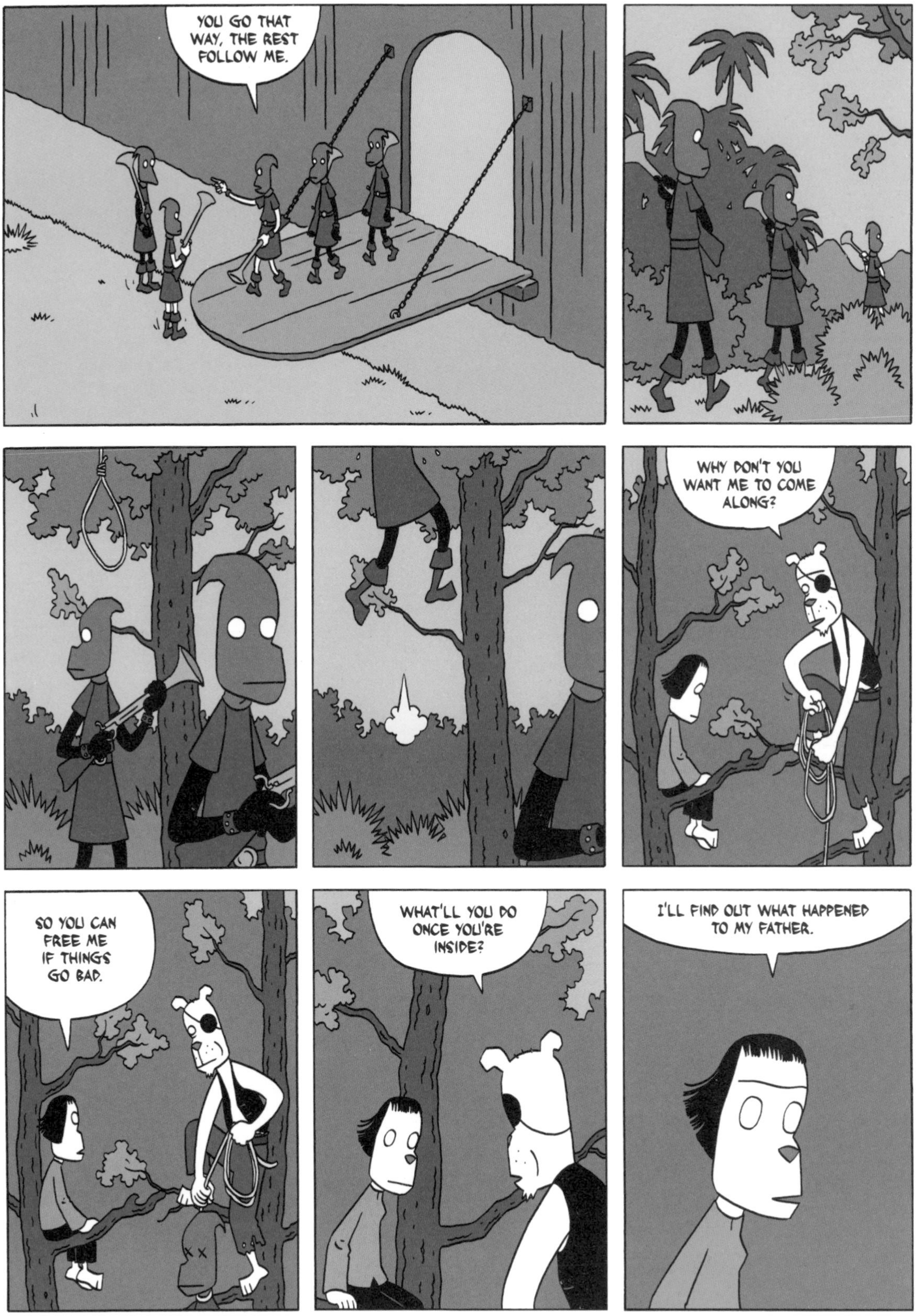
YOU GO THAT WAY, THE REST FOLLOW ME.
WHY DON'T YOU WANT ME TO COME ALONG?
SO YOU CAN FREE ME IF THINGS GO BAD.
WHAT'LL YOU DO ONCE YOU'RE INSIDE?
I'LL FIND OUT WHAT HAPPENED TO MY FATHER.

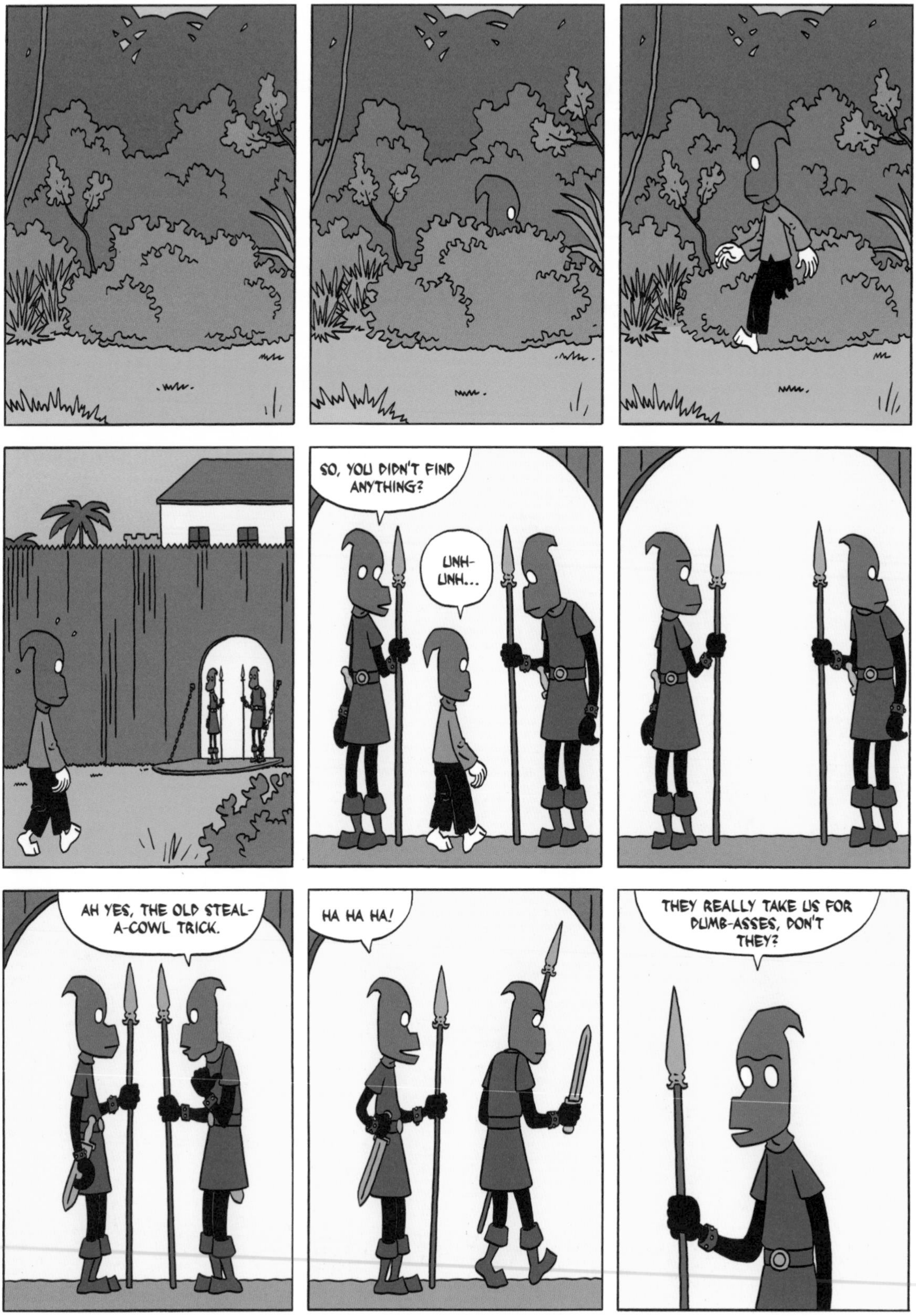
SO, YOU DIDN'T FIND ANYTHING?
UNH-UNH...
AH YES, THE OLD STEAL-A-COWL TRICK.
HA HA HA!
THEY REALLY TAKE US FOR DUMB-ASSES, DON'T THEY?

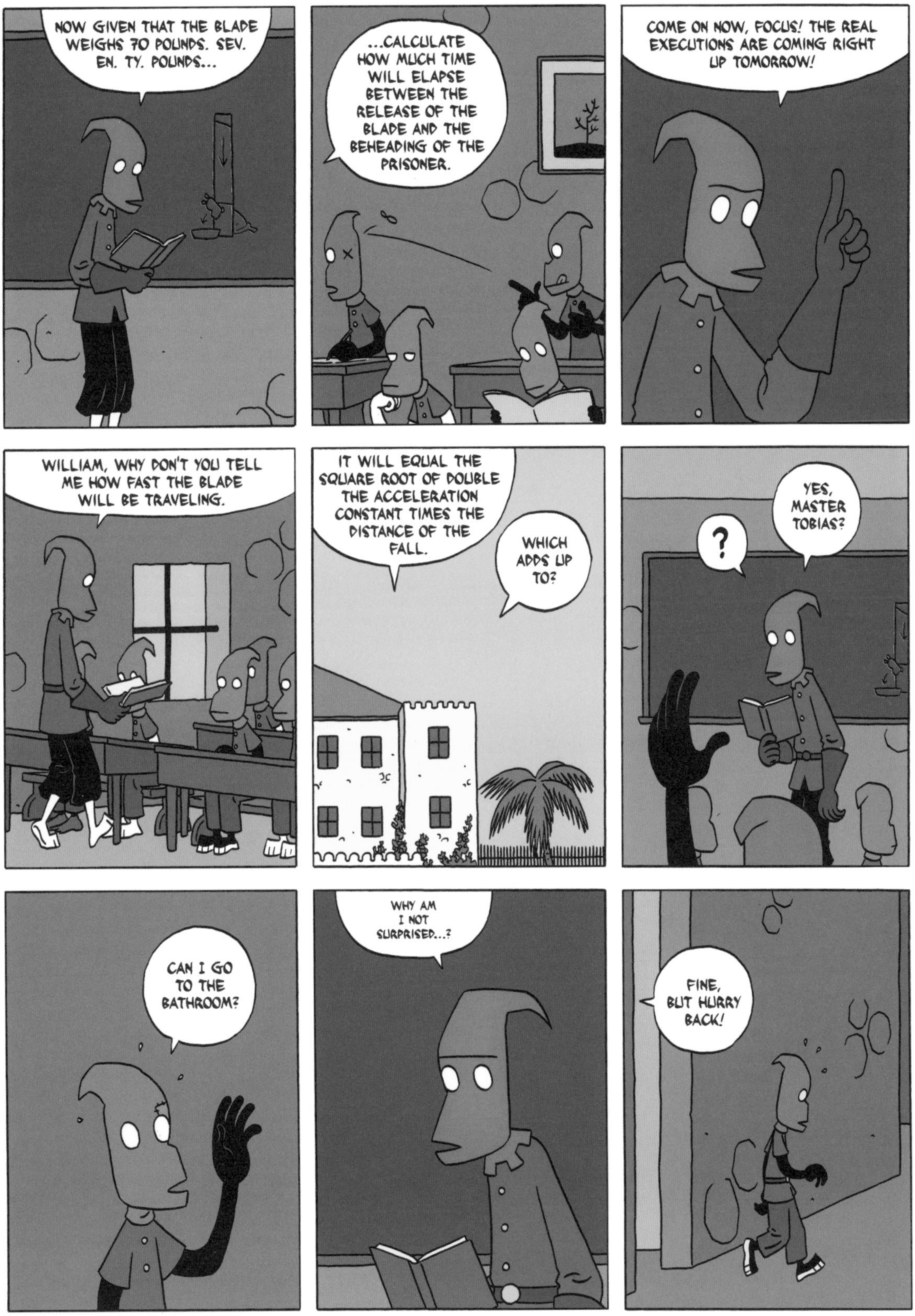
NOW GIVEN THAT THE BLADE WEIGHS 70 POUNDS. SEV. EN. TY. POUNDS...
...CALCULATE HOW MUCH TIME WILL ELAPSE BETWEEN THE RELEASE OF THE BLADE AND THE BEHEADING OF THE PRISONER.
COME ON NOW, FOCUS! THE REAL EXECUTIONS ARE COMING RIGHT UP TOMORROW!
WILLIAM, WHY DON'T YOU TELL ME HOW FAST THE BLADE WILL BE TRAVELING.
IT WILL EQUAL THE SQUARE ROOT OF DOUBLE THE ACCELERATION CONSTANT TIMES THE DISTANCE OF THE FALL.
WHICH ADDS UP TO?
?
YES, MASTER TOBIAS?
CAN I GO TO THE BATHROOM?
WHY AM I NOT SURPRISED...?
FINE, BUT HURRY BACK!

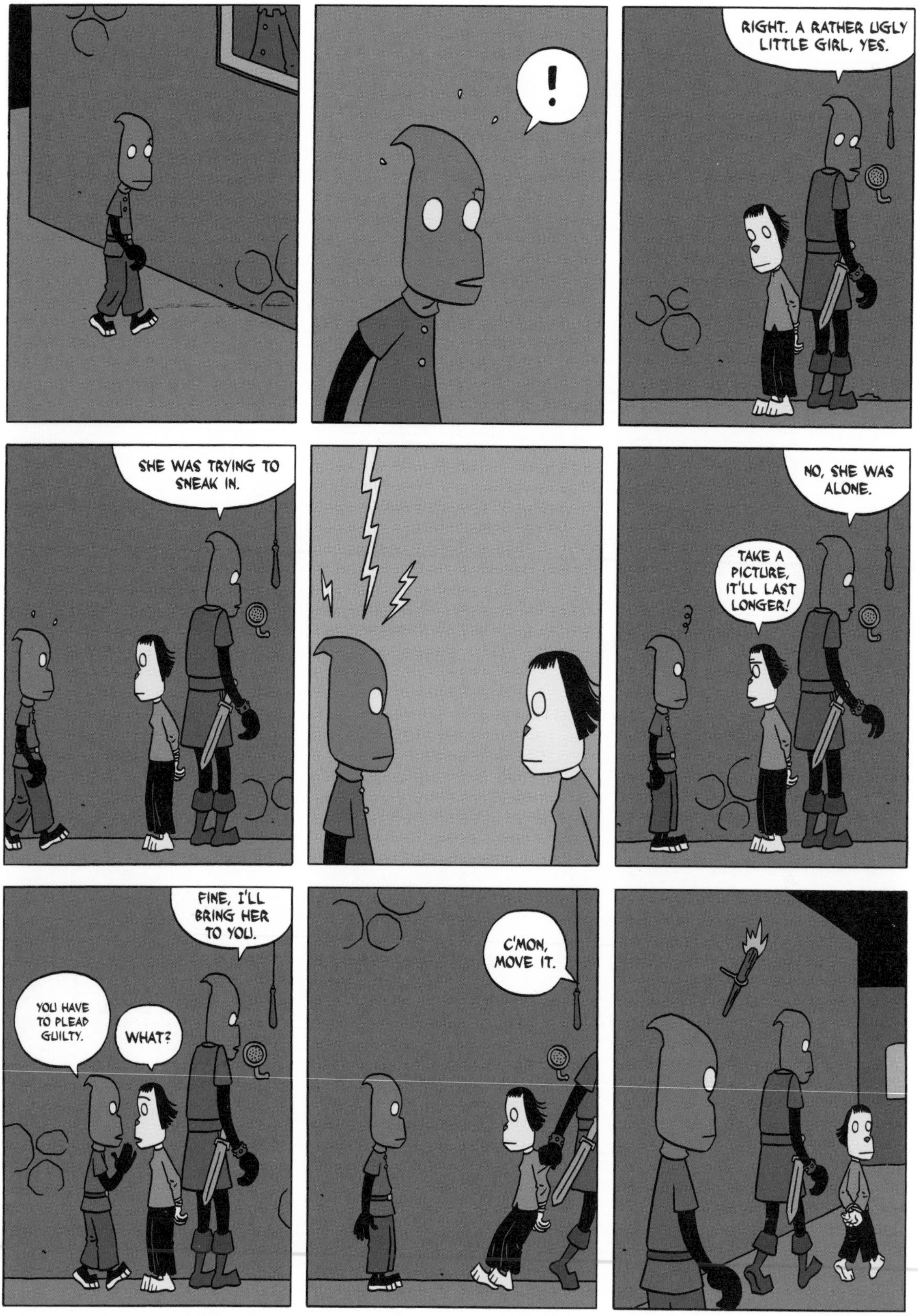
!
RIGHT. A RATHER UGLY LITTLE GIRL, YES.
SHE WAS TRYING TO SNEAK IN.
NO, SHE WAS ALONE.
TAKE A PICTURE, IT'LL LAST LONGER!
FINE, I'LL BRING HER TO YOU.
YOU HAVE TO PLEAD GUILTY.
WHAT?
C'MON, MOVE IT.

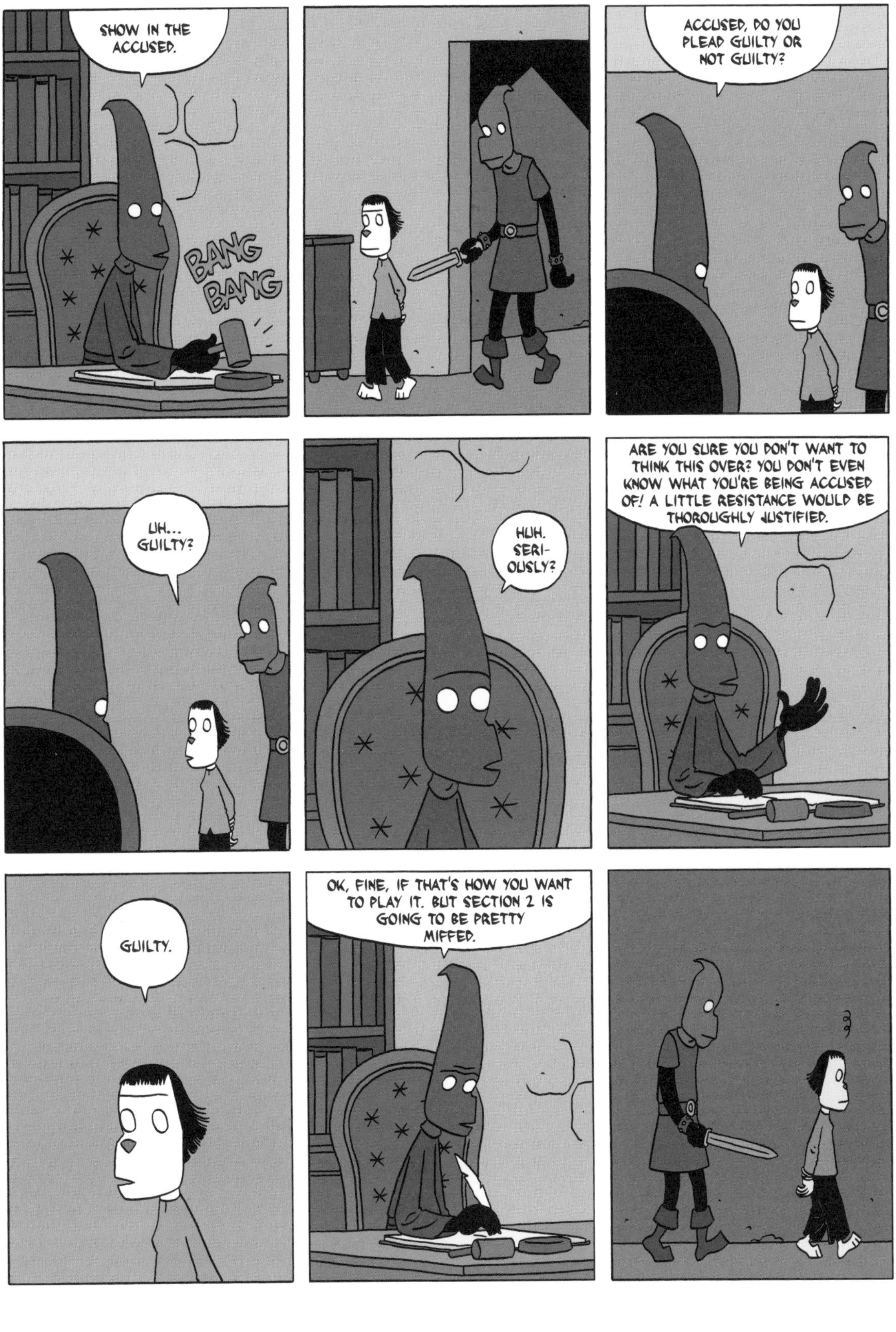
SHOW IN THE ACCUSED.
BANG BANG
ACCUSED, DO YOU PLEAD GUILTY OR NOT GUILTY?
UH... GUILTY?
HUH. SERI-OUSLY?
ARE YOU SURE YOU DON'T WANT TO THINK THIS OVER? YOU DON'T EVEN KNOW WHAT YOU'RE BEING ACCUSED OF! A LITTLE RESISTANCE WOULD BE THOROUGHLY JUSTIFIED.
GUILTY.
OK, FINE, IF THAT'S HOW YOU WANT TO PLAY IT. BUT SECTION 2 IS GOING TO BE PRETTY MIFFED.

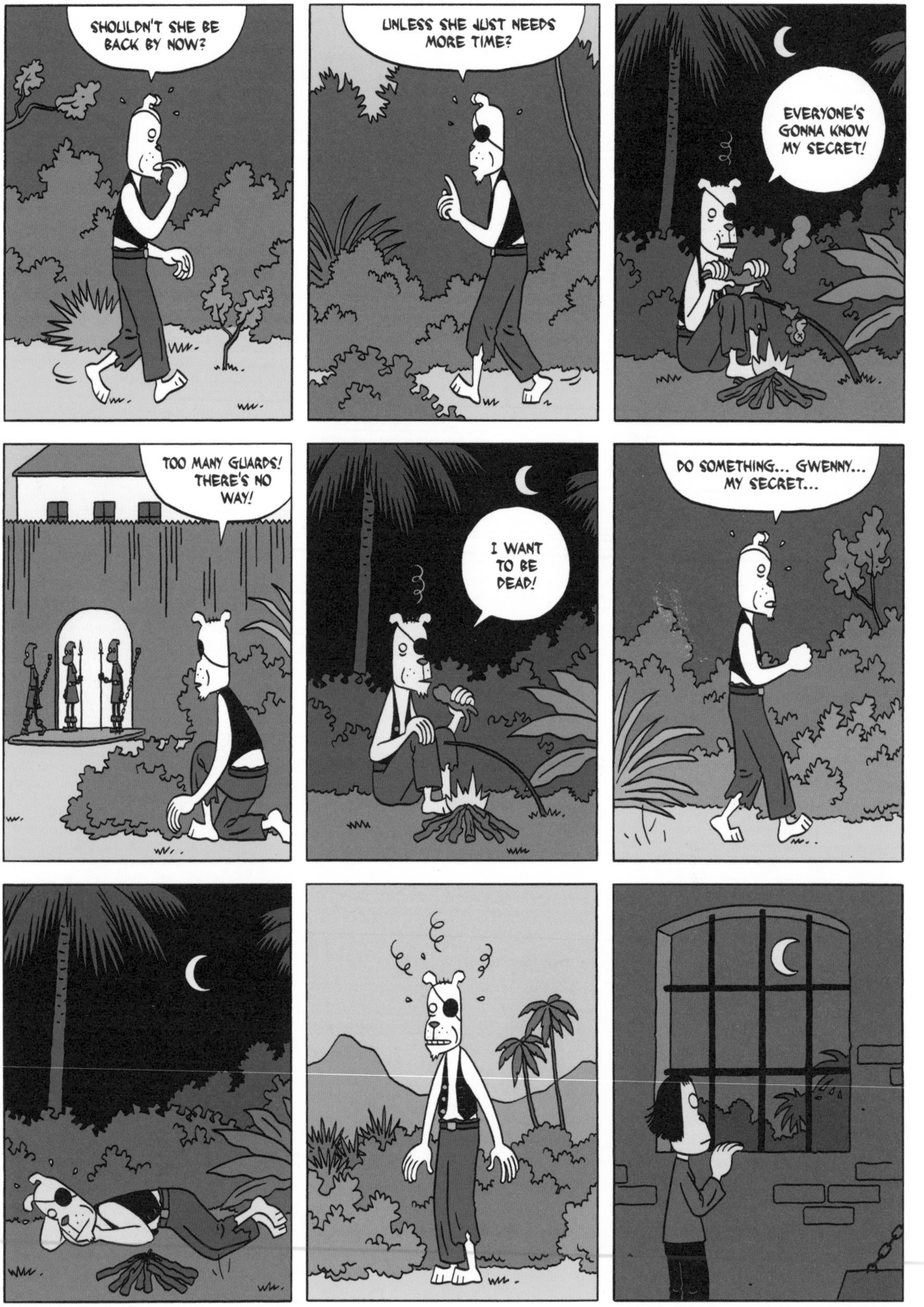
SHOULDN'T SHE BE BACK BY NOW?
UNLESS SHE JUST NEEDS MORE TIME?
EVERYONE'S GONNA KNOW MY SECRET!
TOO MANY GUARDS! THERE'S NO WAY!
I WANT TO BE DEAD!
DO SOMETHING... GWENNY... MY SECRET...

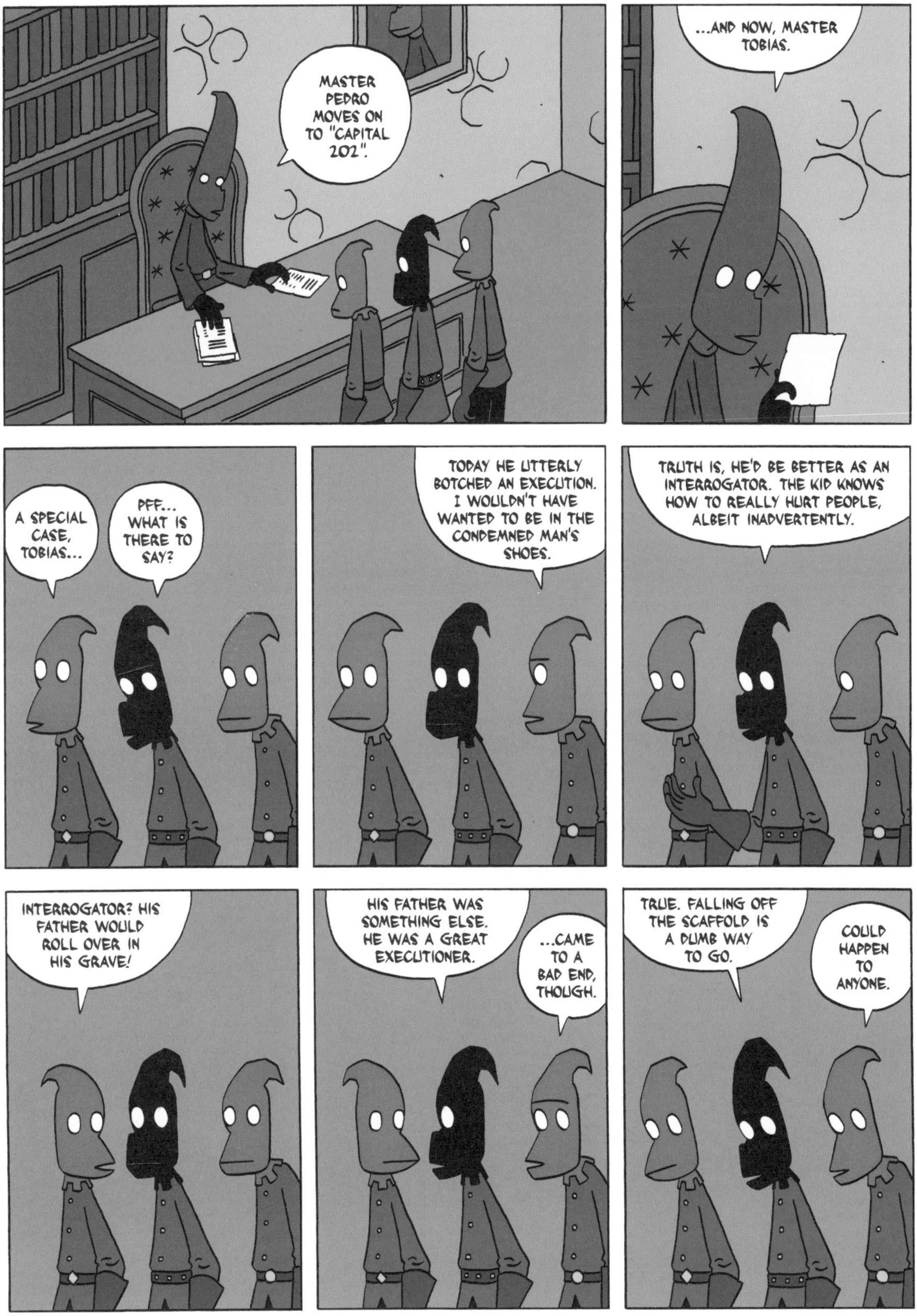
MASTER PEDRO MOVES ON TO "CAPITAL 202".
...AND NOW, MASTER TOBIAS.
A SPECIAL CASE, TOBIAS...
PFF... WHAT IS THERE TO SAY?
TODAY HE UTTERLY BOTCHED AN EXECUTION. I WOULDN'T HAVE WANTED TO BE IN THE CONDEMNED MAN'S SHOES.
TRUTH IS, HE'D BE BETTER AS AN INTERROGATOR. THE KID KNOWS HOW TO REALLY HURT PEOPLE, ALBEIT INADVERTENTLY.
INTERROGATOR? HIS FATHER WOULD ROLL OVER IN HIS GRAVE!
HIS FATHER WAS SOMETHING ELSE. HE WAS A GREAT EXECUTIONER.
...CAME TO A BAD END, THOUGH.
TRUE. FALLING OFF THE SCAFFOLD IS A DUMB WAY TO GO.
COULD HAPPEN TO ANYONE.

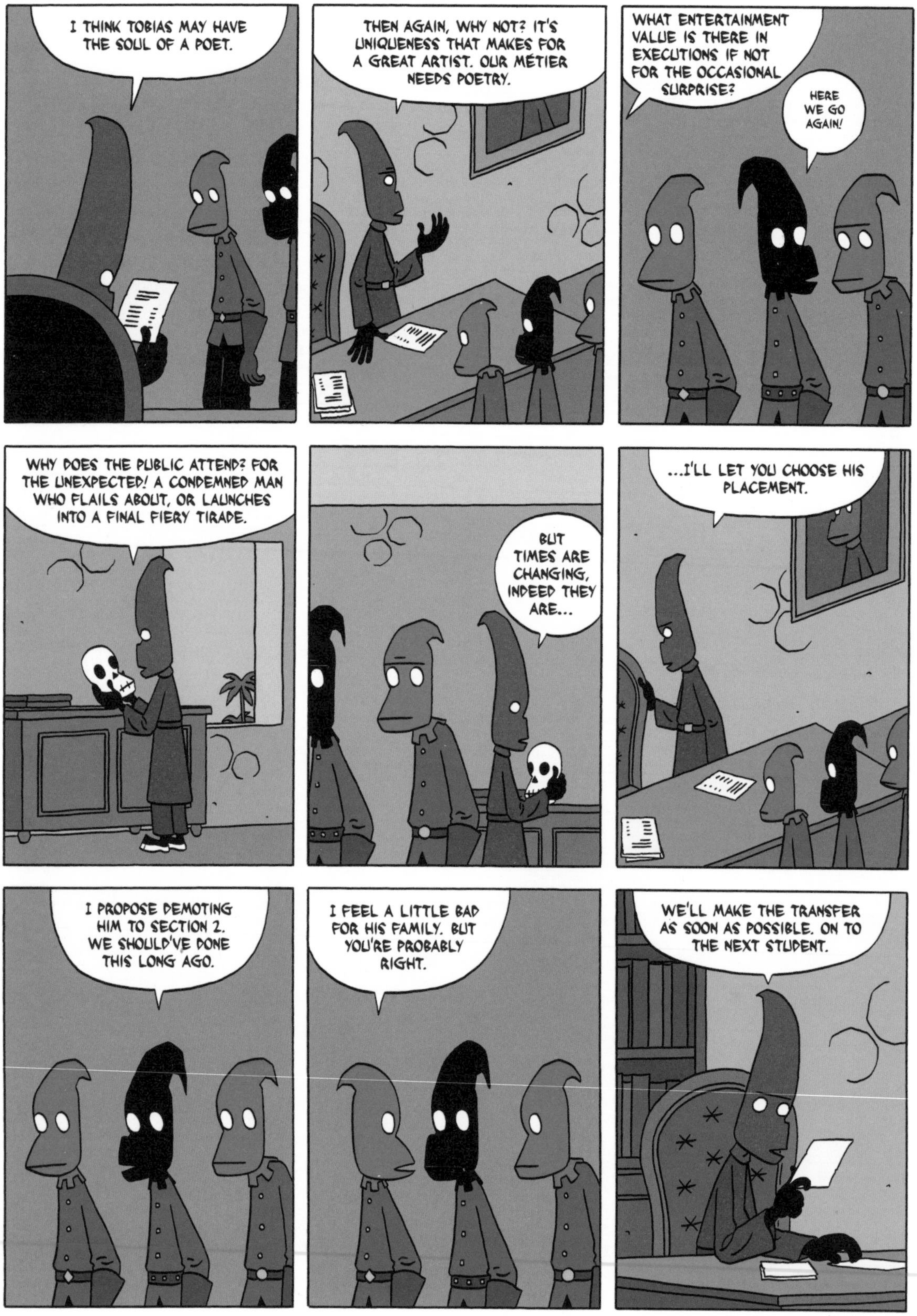
I THINK TOBIAS MAY HAVE THE SOUL OF A POET.
THEN AGAIN, WHY NOT? IT'S UNIQUENESS THAT MAKES FOR A GREAT ARTIST. OUR MÉTIER NEEDS POETRY.
WHAT ENTERTAINMENT VALUE IS THERE IN EXECUTIONS IF NOT FOR THE OCCASIONAL SURPRISE?
HERE WE GO AGAIN!
WHY DOES THE PUBLIC ATTEND? FOR THE UNEXPECTED! A CONDEMNED MAN WHO FLAILS ABOUT, OR LAUNCHES INTO A FINAL FIERY TIRADE.
BUT TIMES ARE CHANGING, INDEED THEY ARE...
...I'LL LET YOU CHOOSE HIS PLACEMENT.
I PROPOSE DEMOTING HIM TO SECTION 2. WE SHOULD'VE DONE THIS LONG AGO.
I FEEL A LITTLE BAD FOR HIS FAMILY. BUT YOU'RE PROBABLY RIGHT.
WE'LL MAKE THE TRANSFER AS SOON AS POSSIBLE. ON TO THE NEXT STUDENT.

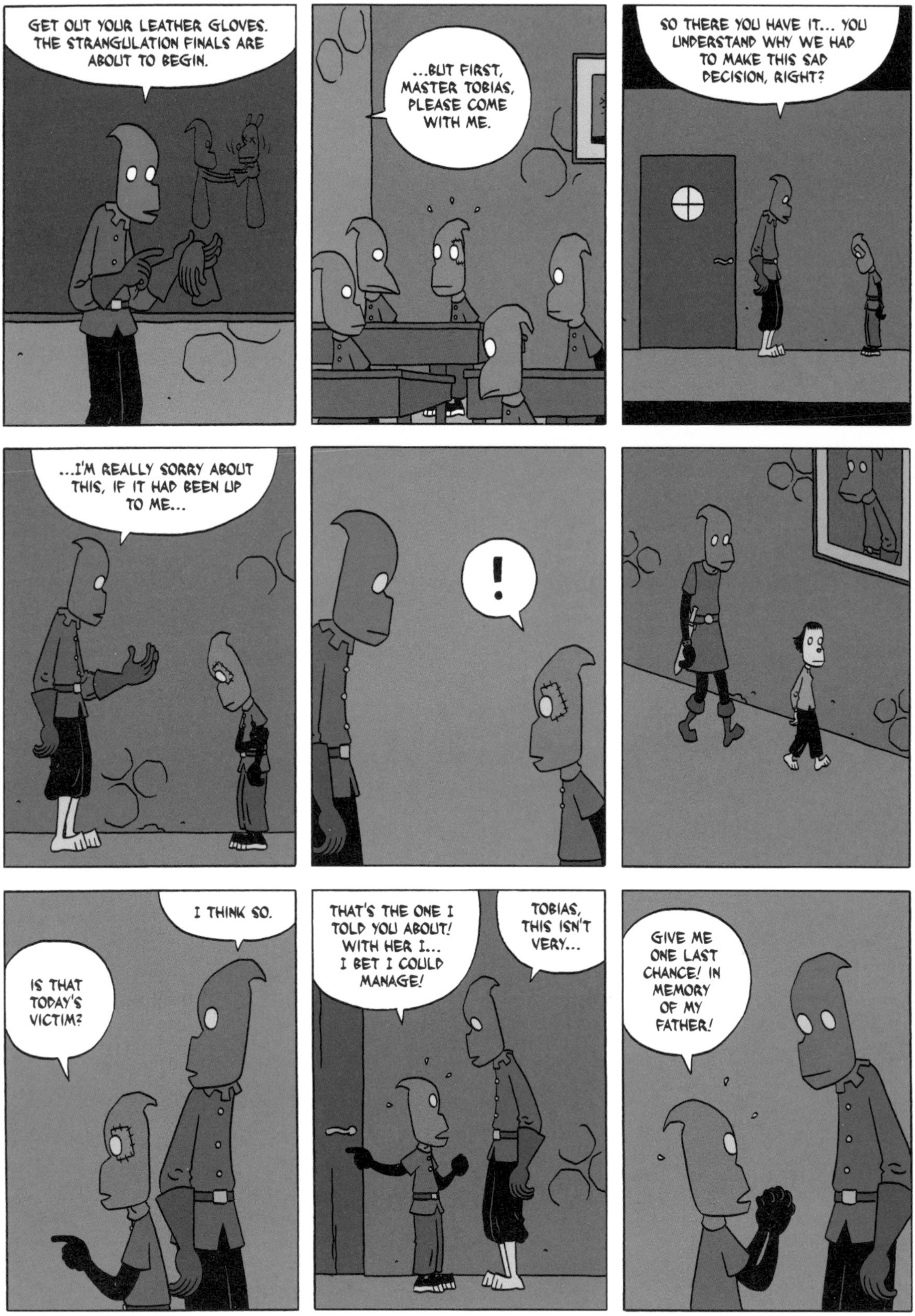
GET OUT YOUR LEATHER GLOVES. THE STRANGULATION FINALS ARE ABOUT TO BEGIN.
...BUT FIRST, MASTER TOBIAS, PLEASE COME WITH ME.
SO THERE YOU HAVE IT... YOU UNDERSTAND WHY WE HAD TO MAKE THIS SAD DECISION, RIGHT?
...I'M REALLY SORRY ABOUT THIS, IF IT HAD BEEN UP TO ME...
!
I THINK SO.
IS THAT TODAY'S VICTIM?
THAT'S THE ONE I TOLD YOU ABOUT! WITH HER I... I BET I COULD MANAGE!
TOBIAS, THIS ISN'T VERY...
GIVE ME ONE LAST CHANCE! IN MEMORY OF MY FATHER!

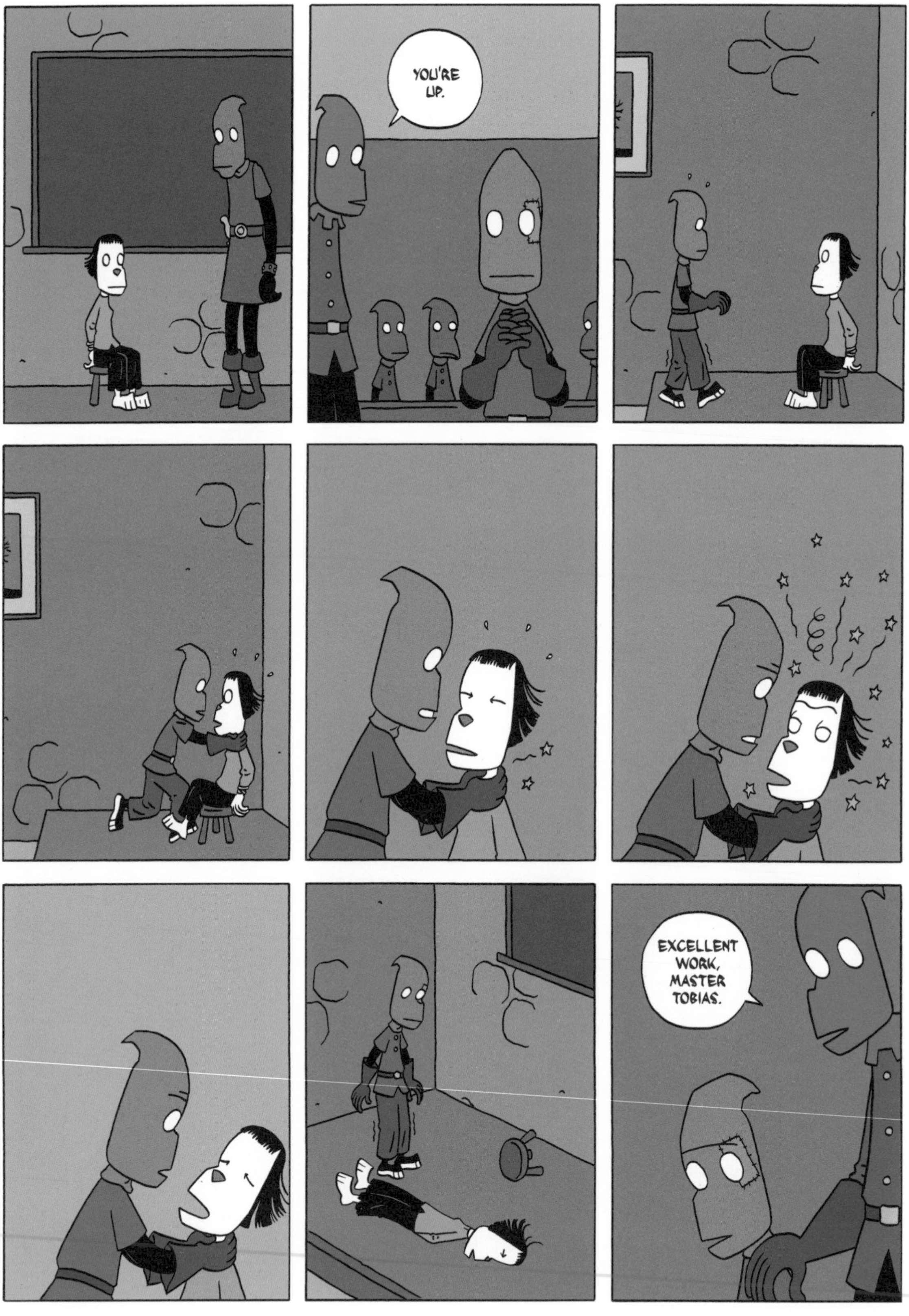
YOU'RE UP.
EXCELLENT WORK, MASTER TOBIAS.

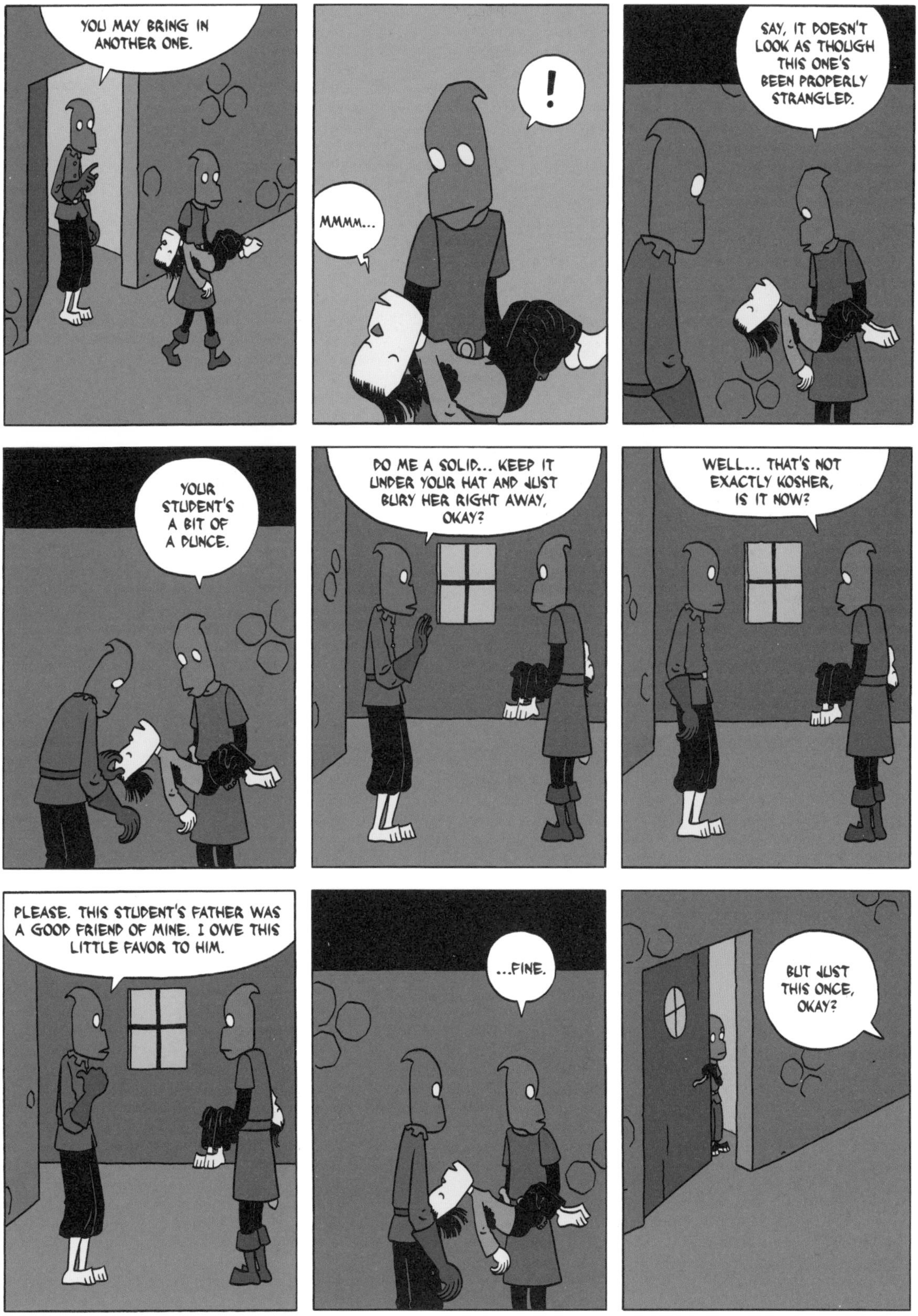
YOU MAY BRING IN ANOTHER ONE.
!
MMMM...
SAY, IT DOESN'T LOOK AS THOUGH THIS ONE'S BEEN PROPERLY STRANGLED.
YOUR STUDENT'S A BIT OF A DUNCE.
DO ME A SOLID... KEEP IT UNDER YOUR HAT AND JUST BURY HER RIGHT AWAY, OKAY?
WELL... THAT'S NOT EXACTLY KOSHER, IS IT NOW?
PLEASE. THIS STUDENT'S FATHER WAS A GOOD FRIEND OF MINE. I OWE THIS LITTLE FAVOR TO HIM.
...FINE.
BUT JUST THIS ONCE, OKAY?

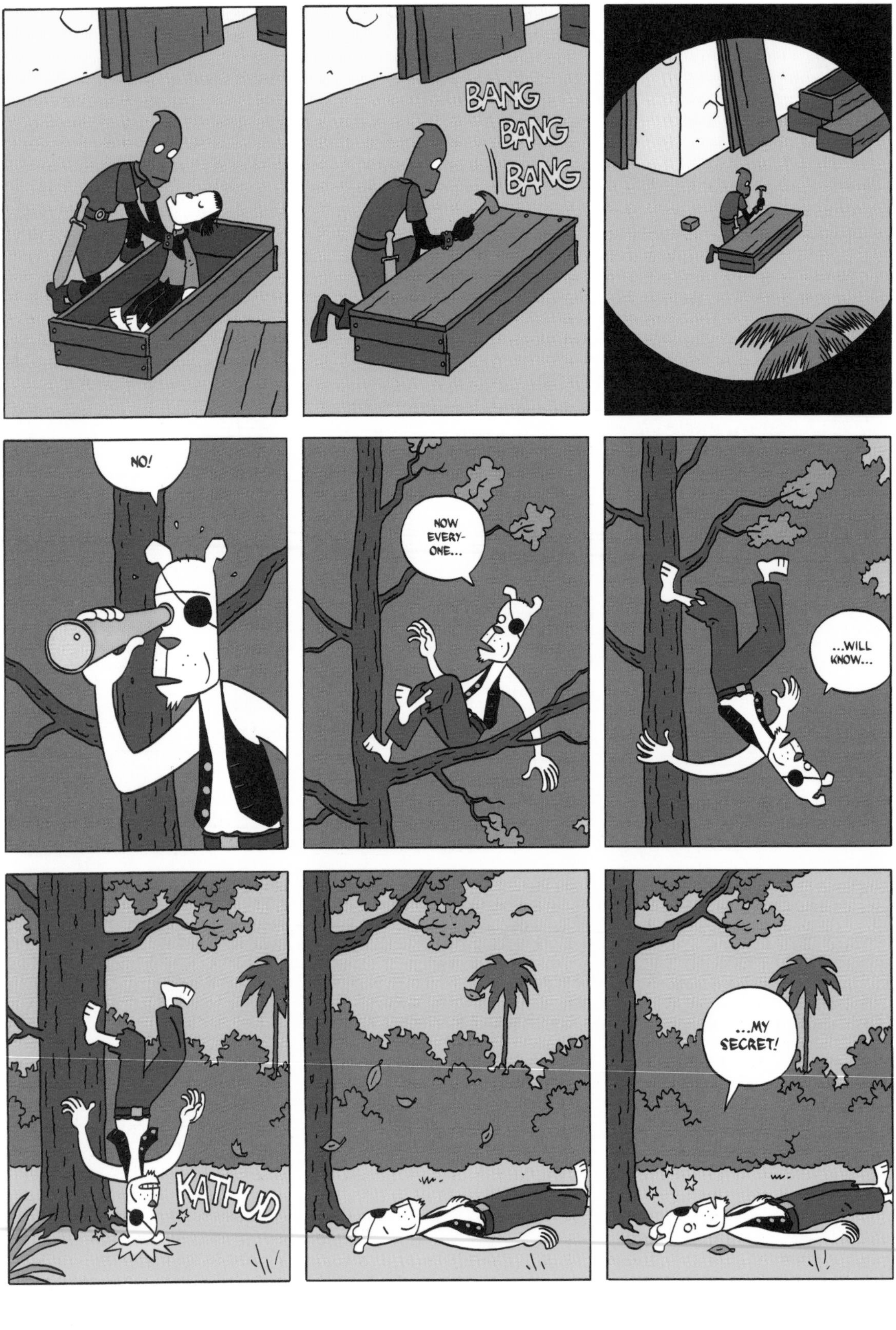
BANG
BANG
BANG
NO!
NOW EVERY-ONE...
...WILL KNOW...
KATHUD
...MY SECRET!

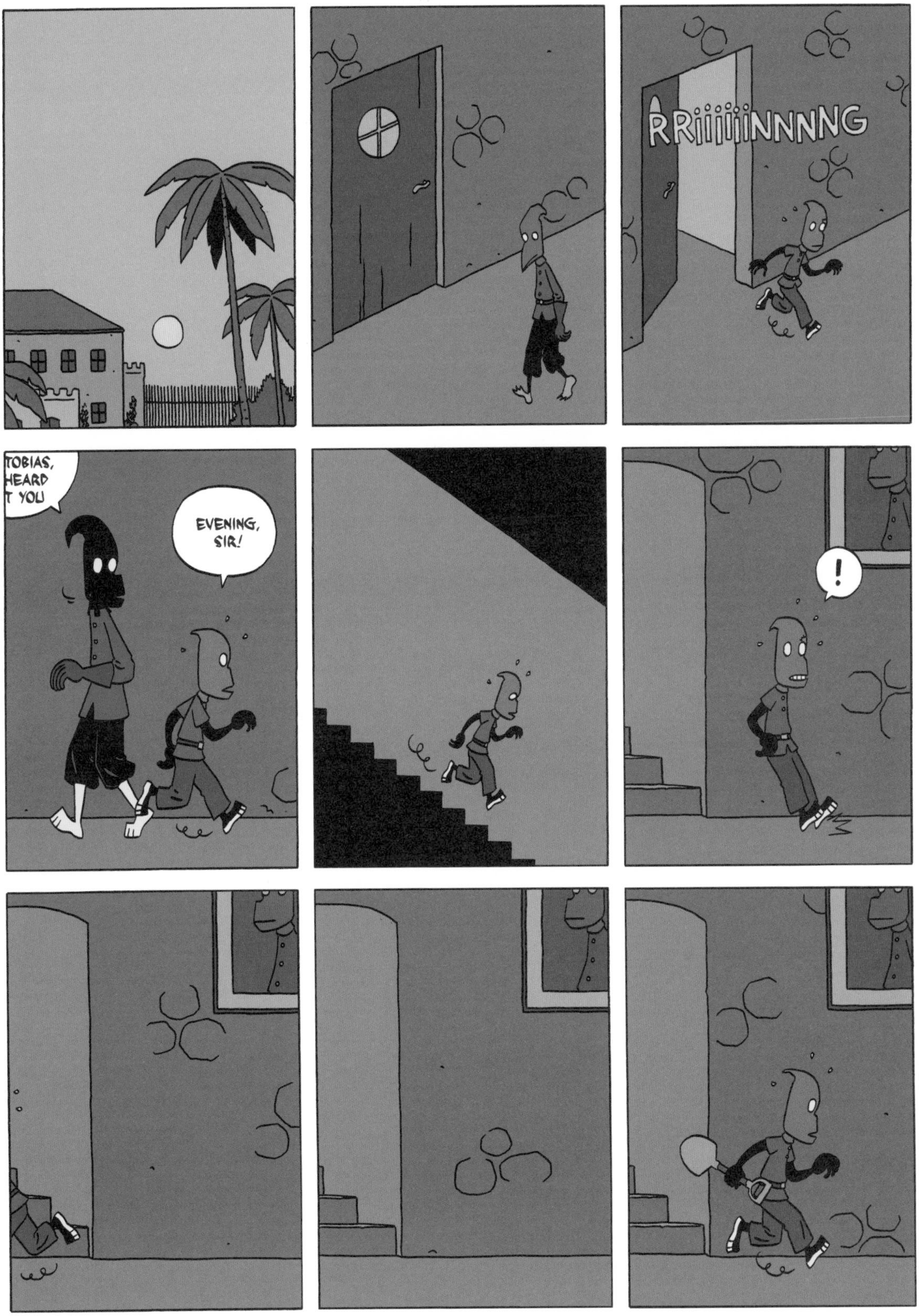
RRiiiiiiNNNNG
TOBIAS,
HEARD
T YOU
EVENING,
SIR!
!

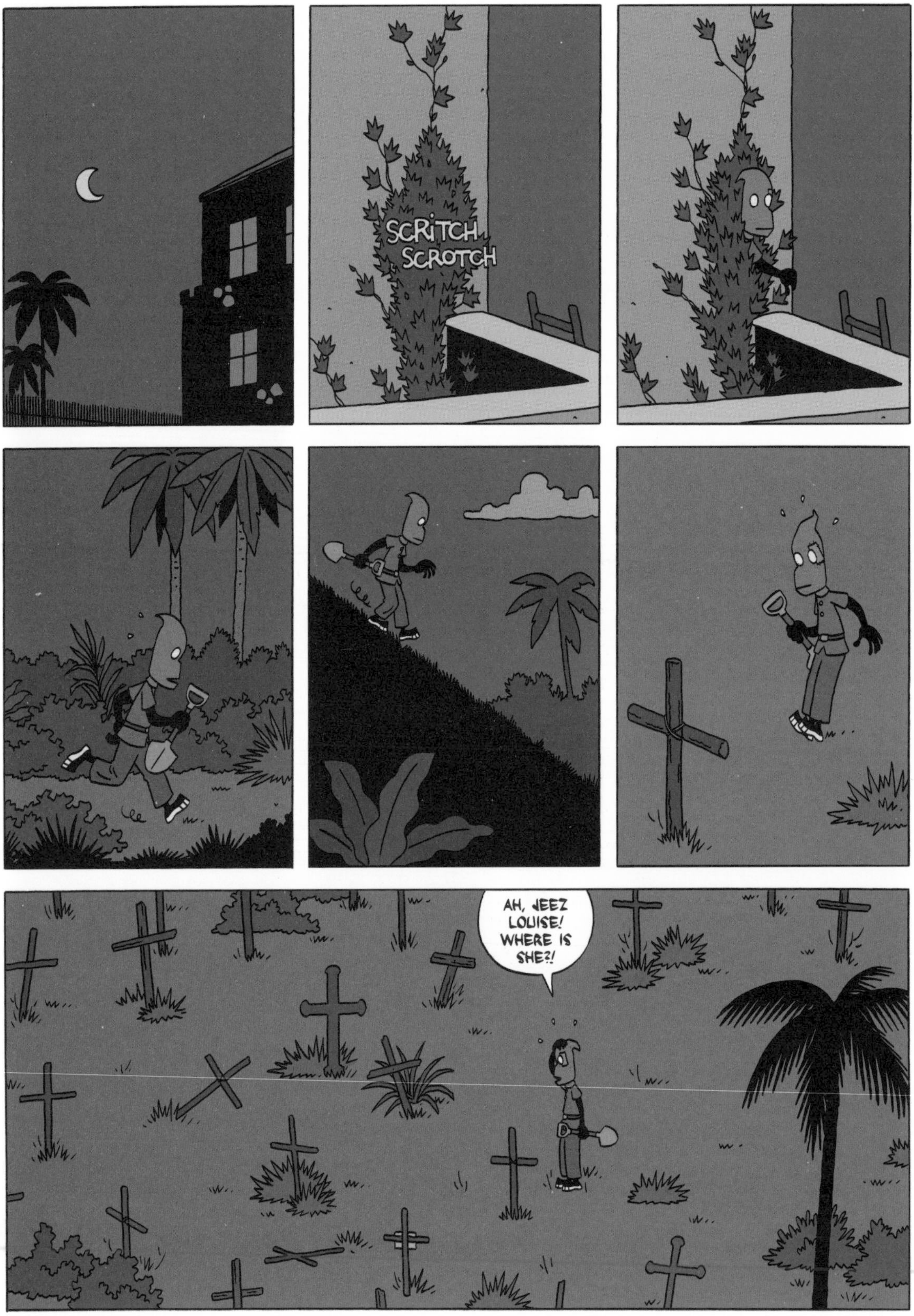
SCRITCH
SCROTCH
AH, JEEZ LOUISE! WHERE IS SHE?!

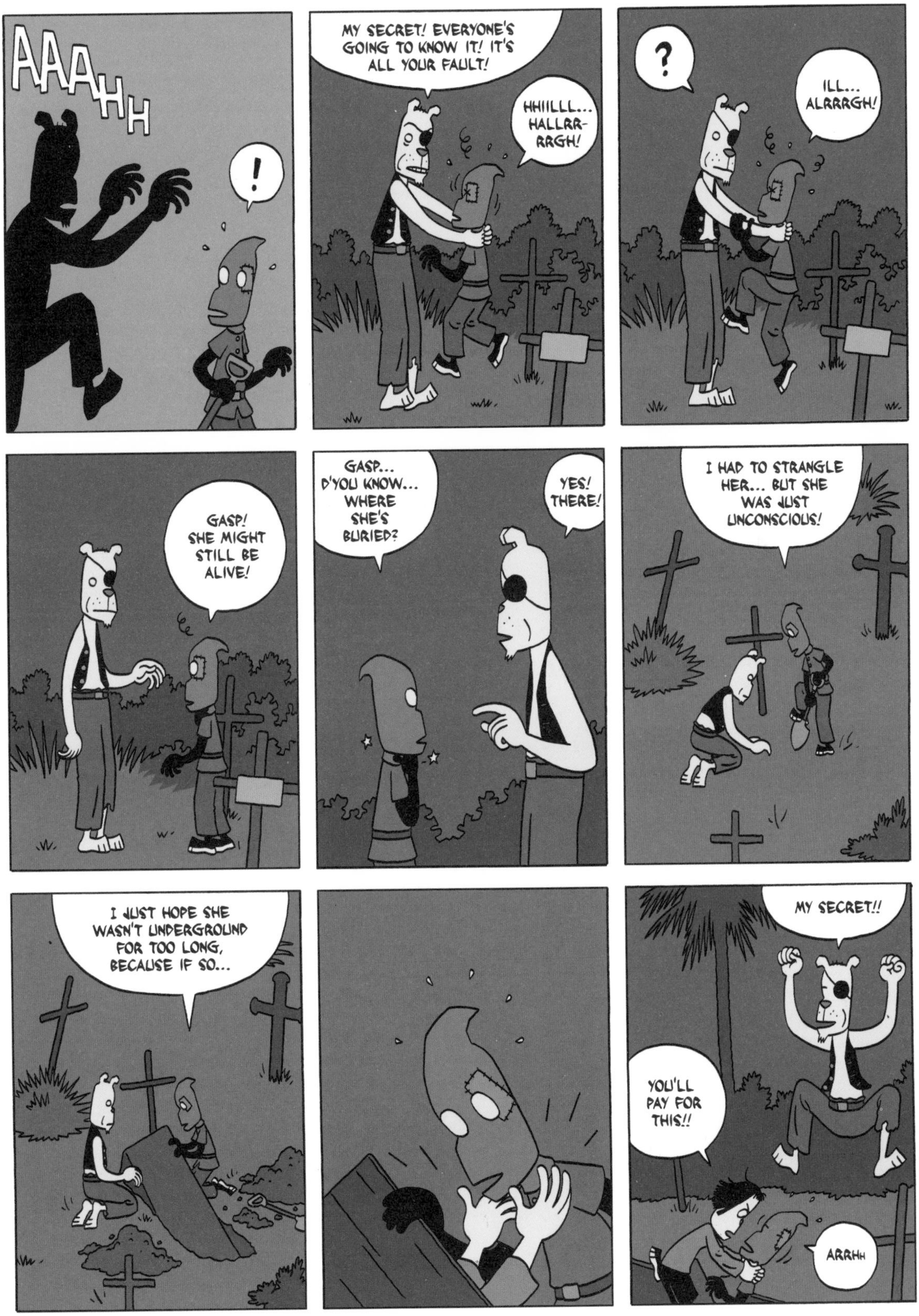
AAAHH
!
MY SECRET! EVERYONE'S GOING TO KNOW IT! IT'S ALL YOUR FAULT!
HHIILLL... HALLRR-RRGH!
?
ILL... ALRRRGH!
GASP! SHE MIGHT STILL BE ALIVE!
GASP... D'YOU KNOW... WHERE SHE'S BURIED?
YES! THERE!
I HAD TO STRANGLE HER... BUT SHE WAS JUST UNCONSCIOUS!
I JUST HOPE SHE WASN'T UNDERGROUND FOR TOO LONG, BECAUSE IF SO...
MY SECRET!!
YOU'LL PAY FOR THIS!!
ARRHH

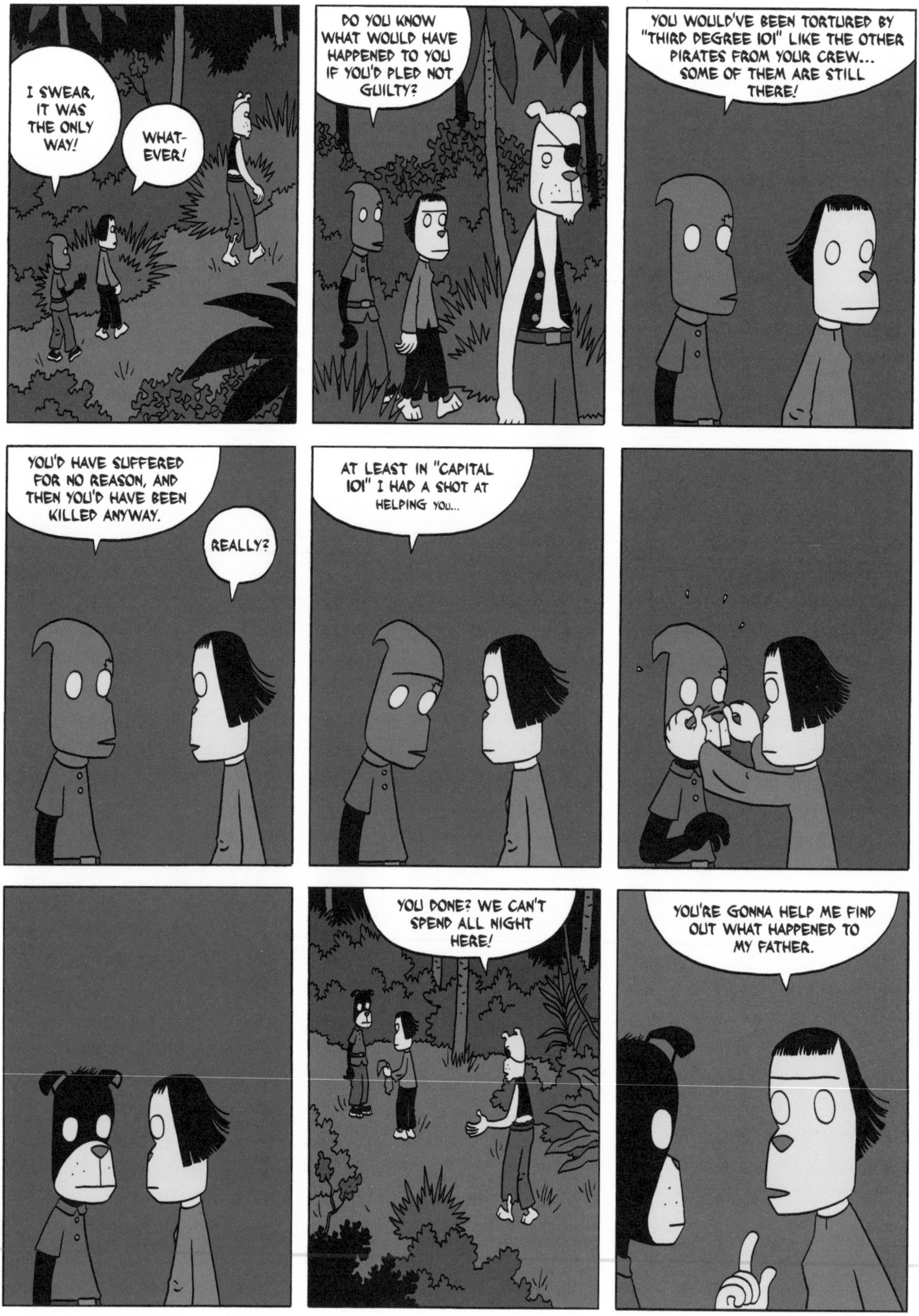
I SWEAR, IT WAS THE ONLY WAY!
WHAT-EVER!
DO YOU KNOW WHAT WOULD HAVE HAPPENED TO YOU IF YOU'D PLED NOT GUILTY?
YOU WOULD'VE BEEN TORTURED BY "THIRD DEGREE 101" LIKE THE OTHER PIRATES FROM YOUR CREW... SOME OF THEM ARE STILL THERE!
YOU'D HAVE SUFFERED FOR NO REASON, AND THEN YOU'D HAVE BEEN KILLED ANYWAY.
REALLY?
AT LEAST IN "CAPITAL 101" I HAD A SHOT AT HELPING YOU...
YOU DONE? WE CAN'T SPEND ALL NIGHT HERE!
YOU'RE GONNA HELP ME FIND OUT WHAT HAPPENED TO MY FATHER.

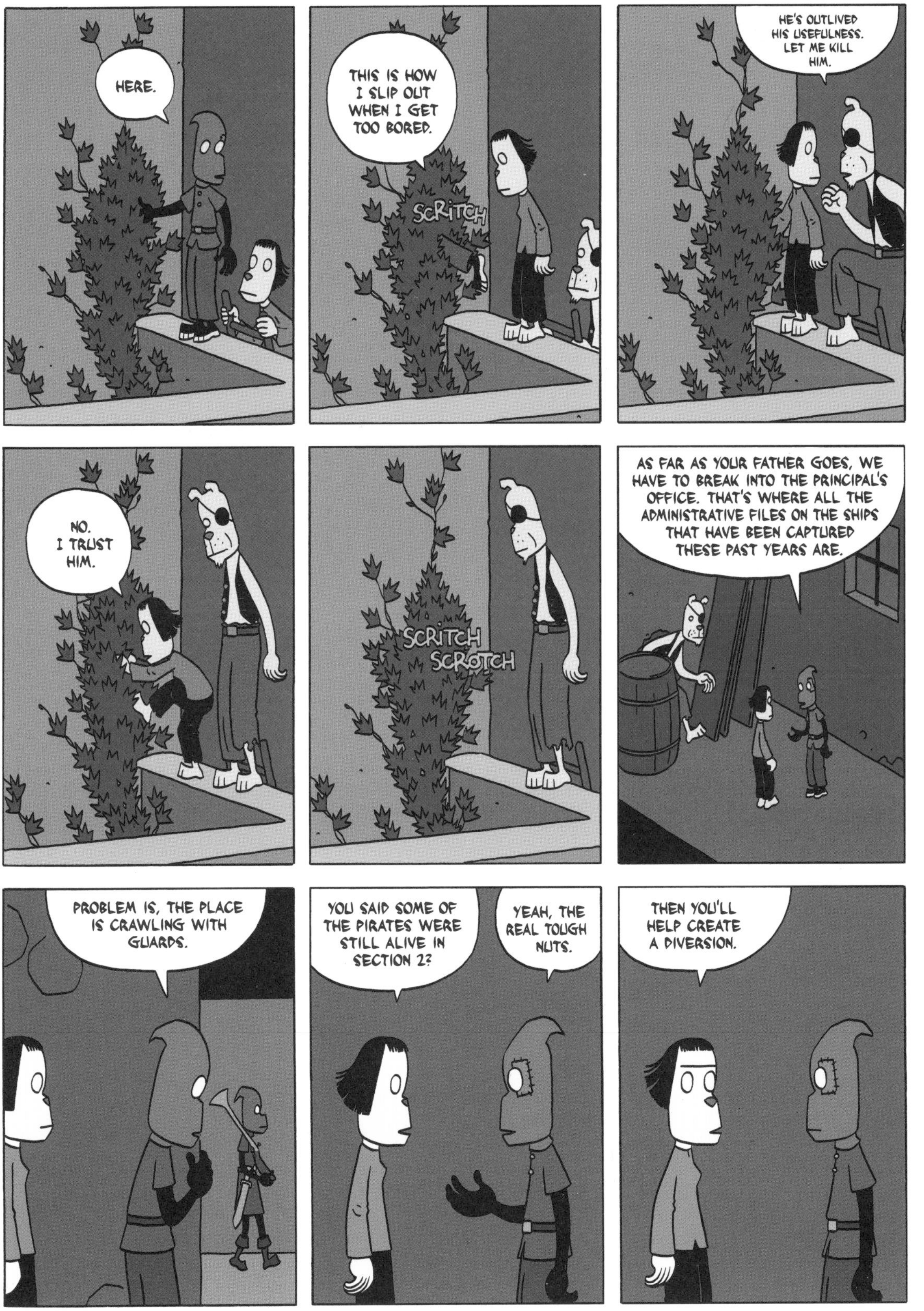
HERE.
THIS IS HOW I SLIP OUT WHEN I GET TOO BORED.
SCRITCH
HE'S OUTLIVED HIS USEFULNESS. LET ME KILL HIM.
NO. I TRUST HIM.
SCRITCH
SCROTCH
AS FAR AS YOUR FATHER GOES, WE HAVE TO BREAK INTO THE PRINCIPAL'S OFFICE. THAT'S WHERE ALL THE ADMINISTRATIVE FILES ON THE SHIPS THAT HAVE BEEN CAPTURED THESE PAST YEARS ARE.
PROBLEM IS, THE PLACE IS CRAWLING WITH GUARDS.
YOU SAID SOME OF THE PIRATES WERE STILL ALIVE IN SECTION 2?
YEAH, THE REAL TOUGH NUTS.
THEN YOU'LL HELP CREATE A DIVERSION.

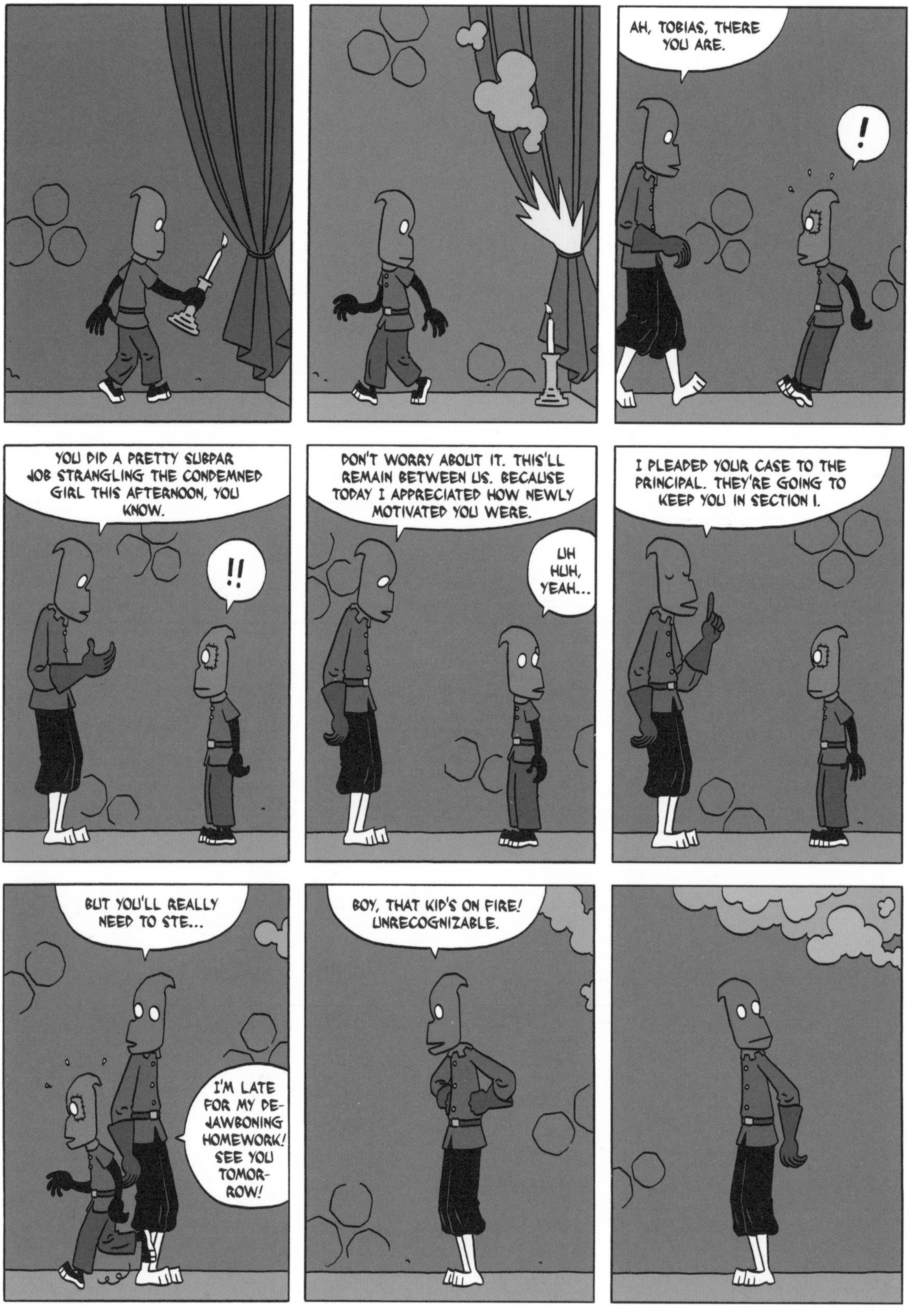
AH, TOBIAS, THERE YOU ARE.
!
YOU DID A PRETTY SUBPAR JOB STRANGLING THE CONDEMNED GIRL THIS AFTERNOON, YOU KNOW.
!!
DON'T WORRY ABOUT IT. THIS'LL REMAIN BETWEEN US. BECAUSE TODAY I APPRECIATED HOW NEWLY MOTIVATED YOU WERE.
UH HUH, YEAH...
I PLEADED YOUR CASE TO THE PRINCIPAL. THEY'RE GOING TO KEEP YOU IN SECTION I.
BUT YOU'LL REALLY NEED TO STE...
I'M LATE FOR MY DE-JAWBONING HOMEWORK! SEE YOU TOMOR-ROW!
BOY, THAT KID'S ON FIRE! UNRECOGNIZABLE.

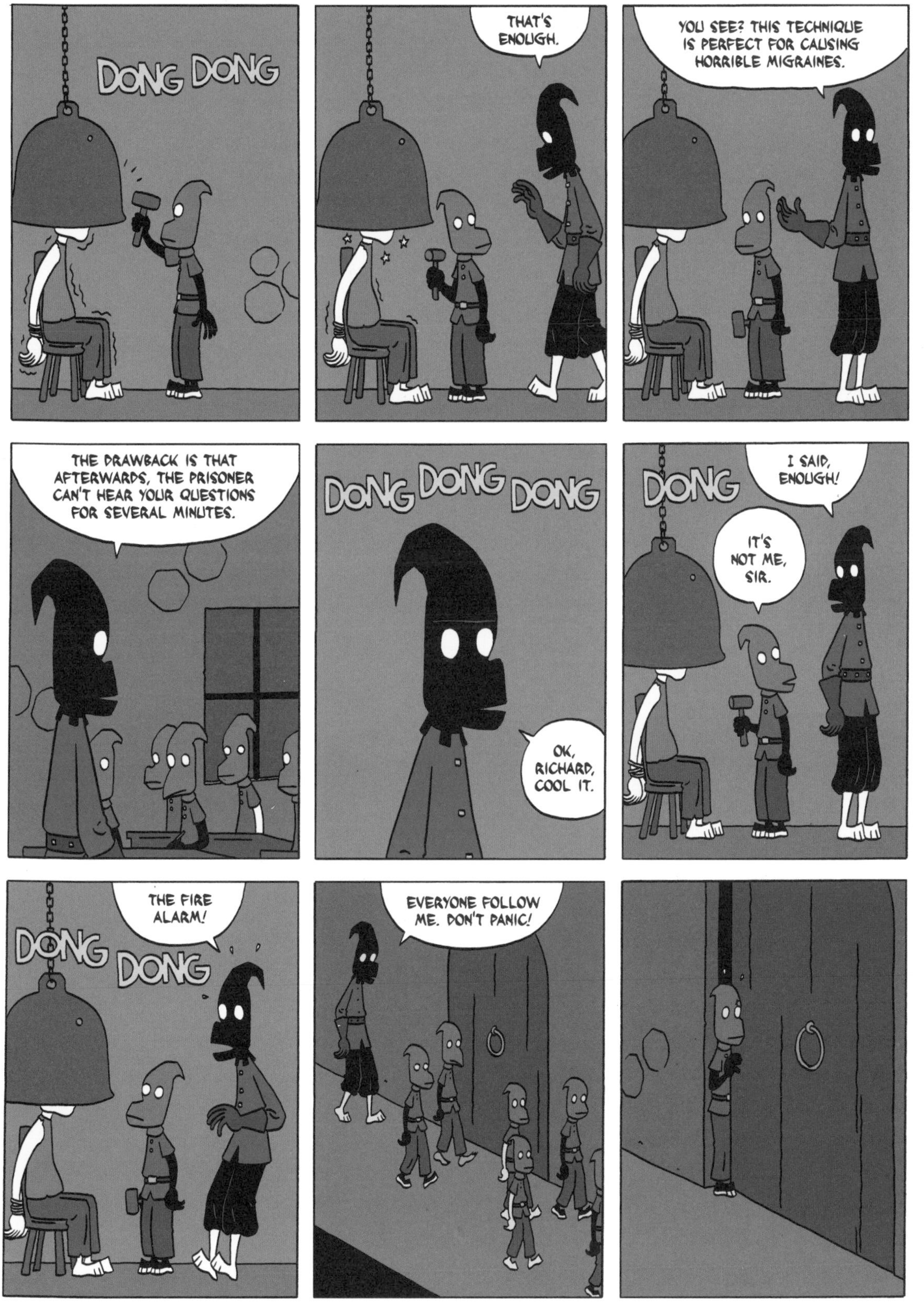
DONG DONG
THAT'S ENOUGH.
YOU SEE? THIS TECHNIQUE IS PERFECT FOR CAUSING HORRIBLE MIGRAINES.
THE DRAWBACK IS THAT AFTERWARDS, THE PRISONER CAN'T HEAR YOUR QUESTIONS FOR SEVERAL MINUTES.
DONG DONG DONG
OK, RICHARD, COOL IT.
DONG
I SAID, ENOUGH!
IT'S NOT ME, SIR.
THE FIRE ALARM!
DONG DONG
EVERYONE FOLLOW ME. DON'T PANIC!

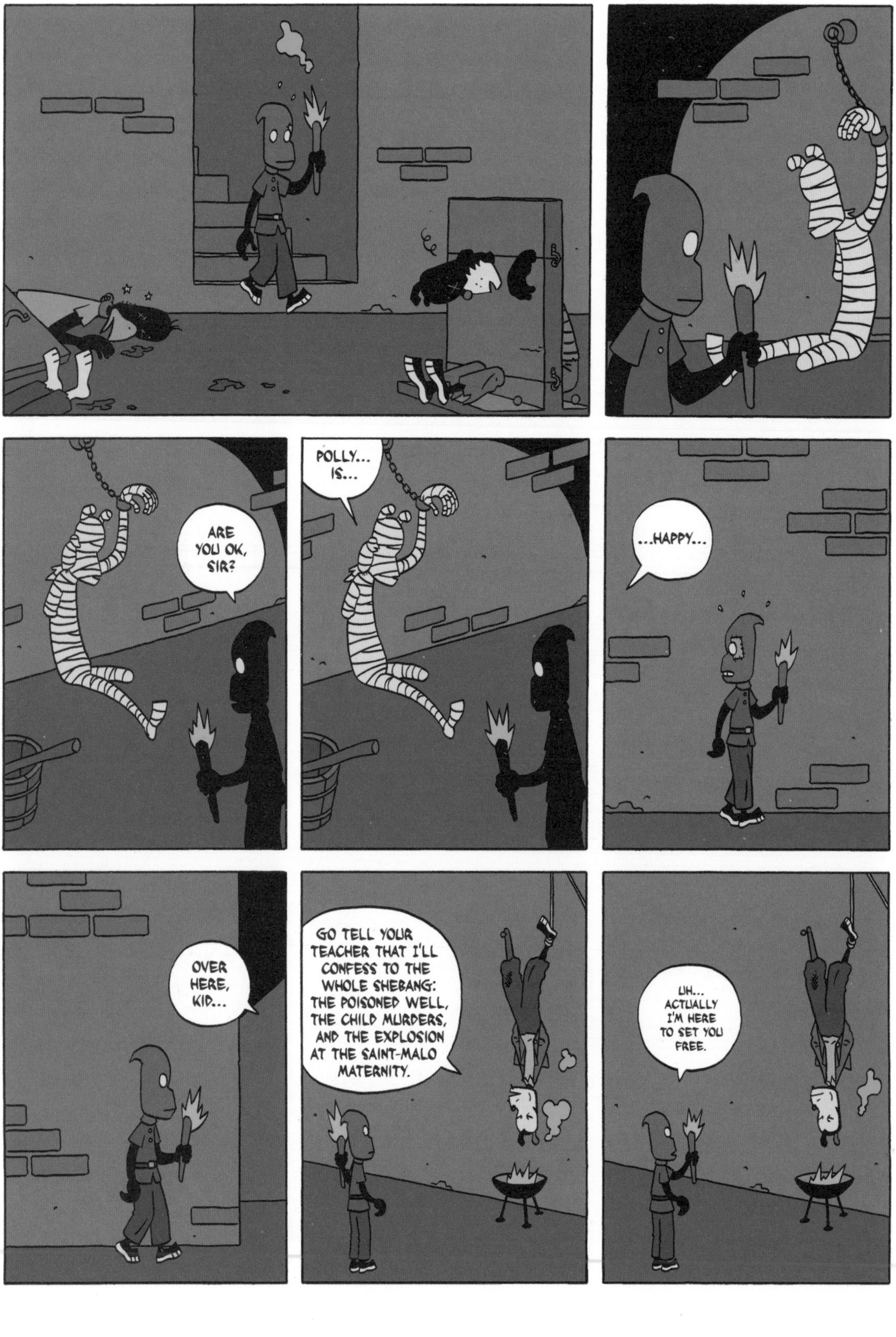
ARE YOU OK, SIR?
POLLY... IS...
...HAPPY...
OVER HERE, KID...
GO TELL YOUR TEACHER THAT I'LL CONFESS TO THE WHOLE SHEBANG: THE POISONED WELL, THE CHILD MURDERS, AND THE EXPLOSION AT THE SAINT-MALO MATERNITY.
UH... ACTUALLY I'M HERE TO SET YOU FREE.

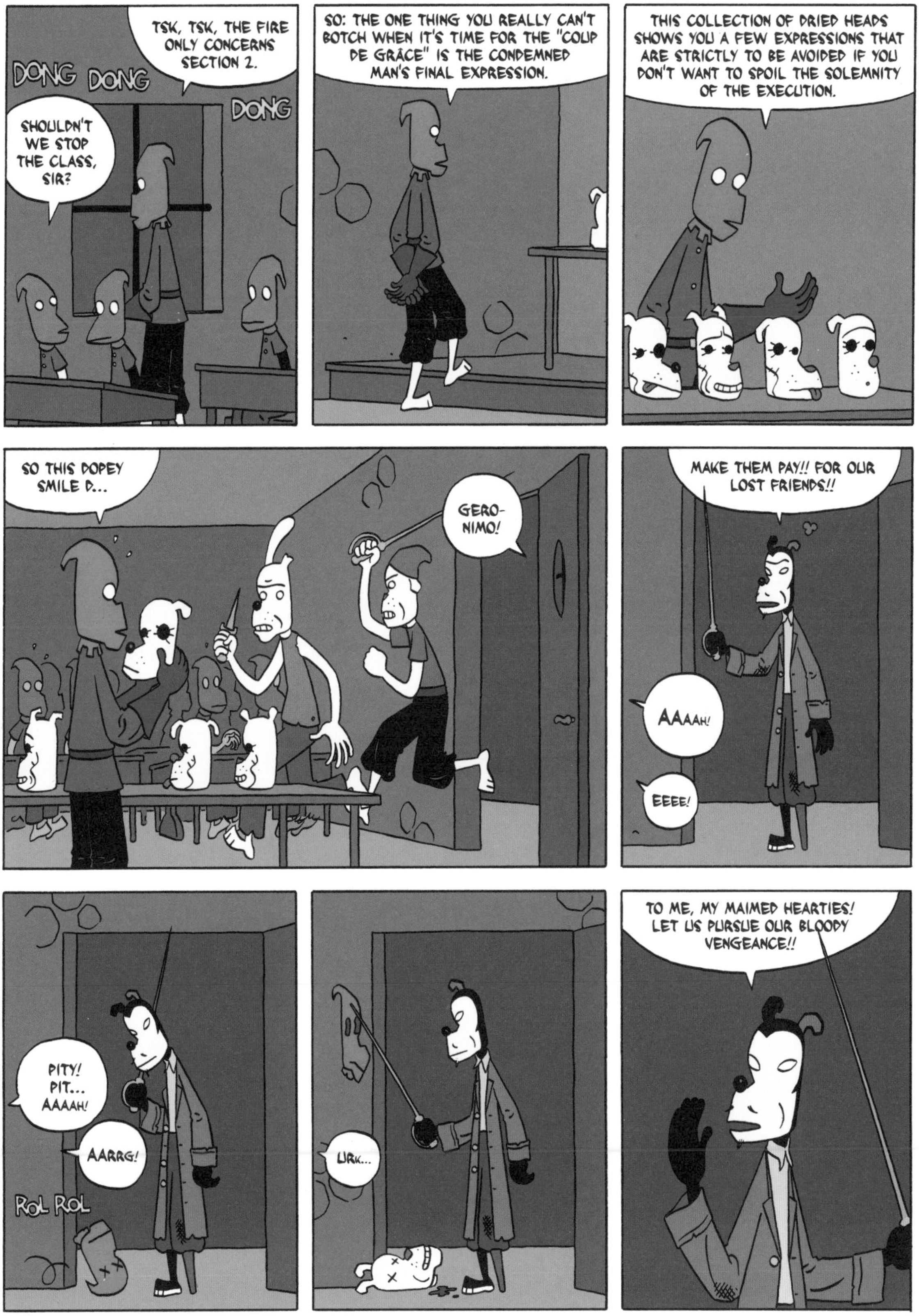
DONG DONG
TSK, TSK, THE FIRE ONLY CONCERNS SECTION 2.
DONG
SHOULDN'T WE STOP THE CLASS, SIR?
SO: THE ONE THING YOU REALLY CAN'T BOTCH WHEN IT'S TIME FOR THE "COUP DE GRÂCE" IS THE CONDEMNED MAN'S FINAL EXPRESSION.
THIS COLLECTION OF DRIED HEADS SHOWS YOU A FEW EXPRESSIONS THAT ARE STRICTLY TO BE AVOIDED IF YOU DON'T WANT TO SPOIL THE SOLEMNITY OF THE EXECUTION.
SO THIS DOPEY SMILE D...
GERO-NIMO!
MAKE THEM PAY!! FOR OUR LOST FRIENDS!!
AAAAH!
EEEE!
PITY! PIT... AAAAH!
AARRG!
ROL ROL
URK...
TO ME, MY MAIMED HEARTIES! LET US PURSUE OUR BLOODY VENGEANCE!!

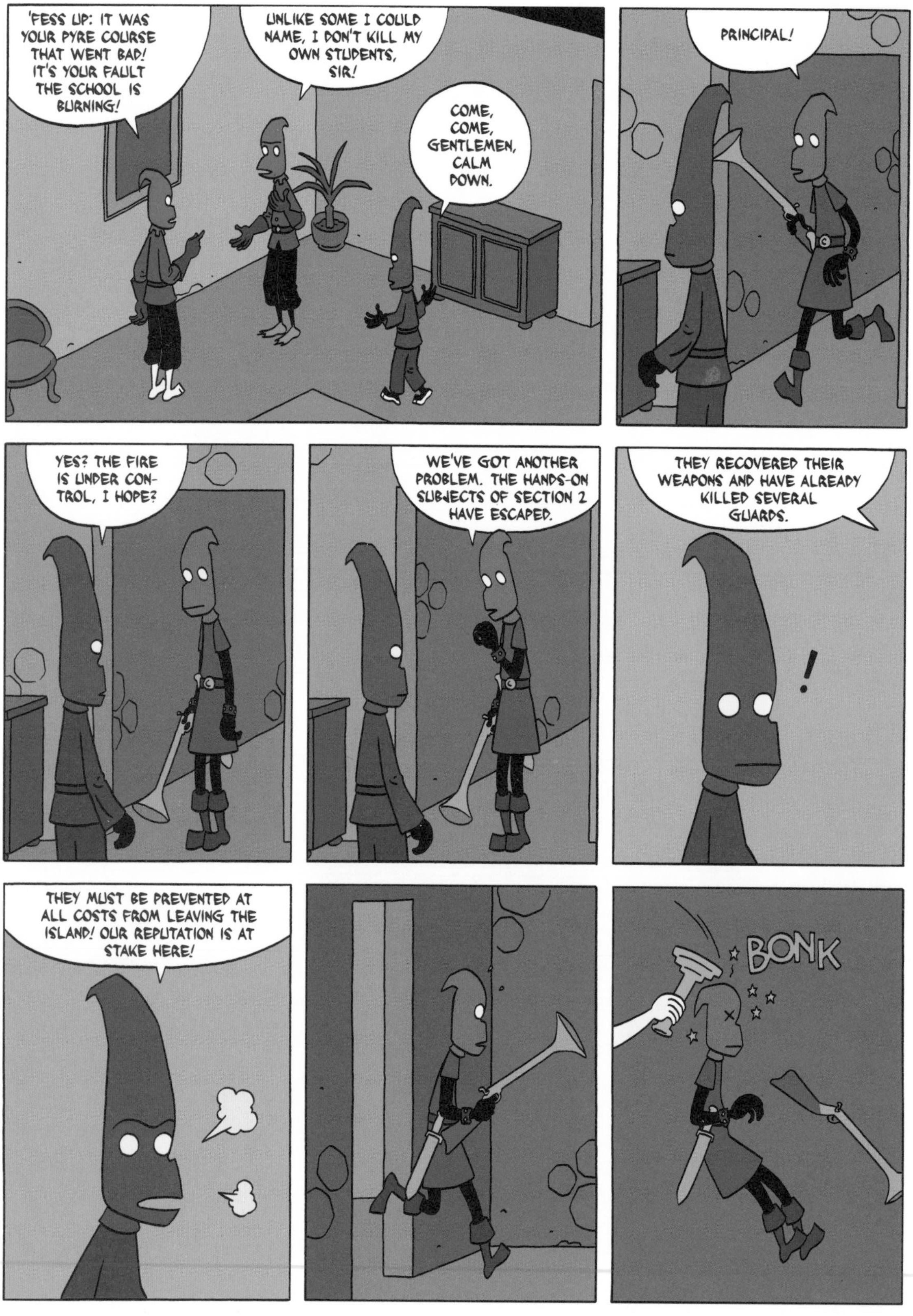
'FESS UP: IT WAS YOUR PYRE COURSE THAT WENT BAD! IT'S YOUR FAULT THE SCHOOL IS BURNING!
UNLIKE SOME I COULD NAME, I DON'T KILL MY OWN STUDENTS, SIR!
COME, COME, GENTLEMEN, CALM DOWN.
PRINCIPAL!
YES? THE FIRE IS UNDER CON-TROL, I HOPE?
WE'VE GOT ANOTHER PROBLEM. THE HANDS-ON SUBJECTS OF SECTION 2 HAVE ESCAPED.
THEY RECOVERED THEIR WEAPONS AND HAVE ALREADY KILLED SEVERAL GUARDS.
!
THEY MUST BE PREVENTED AT ALL COSTS FROM LEAVING THE ISLAND! OUR REPUTATION IS AT STAKE HERE!
BONK

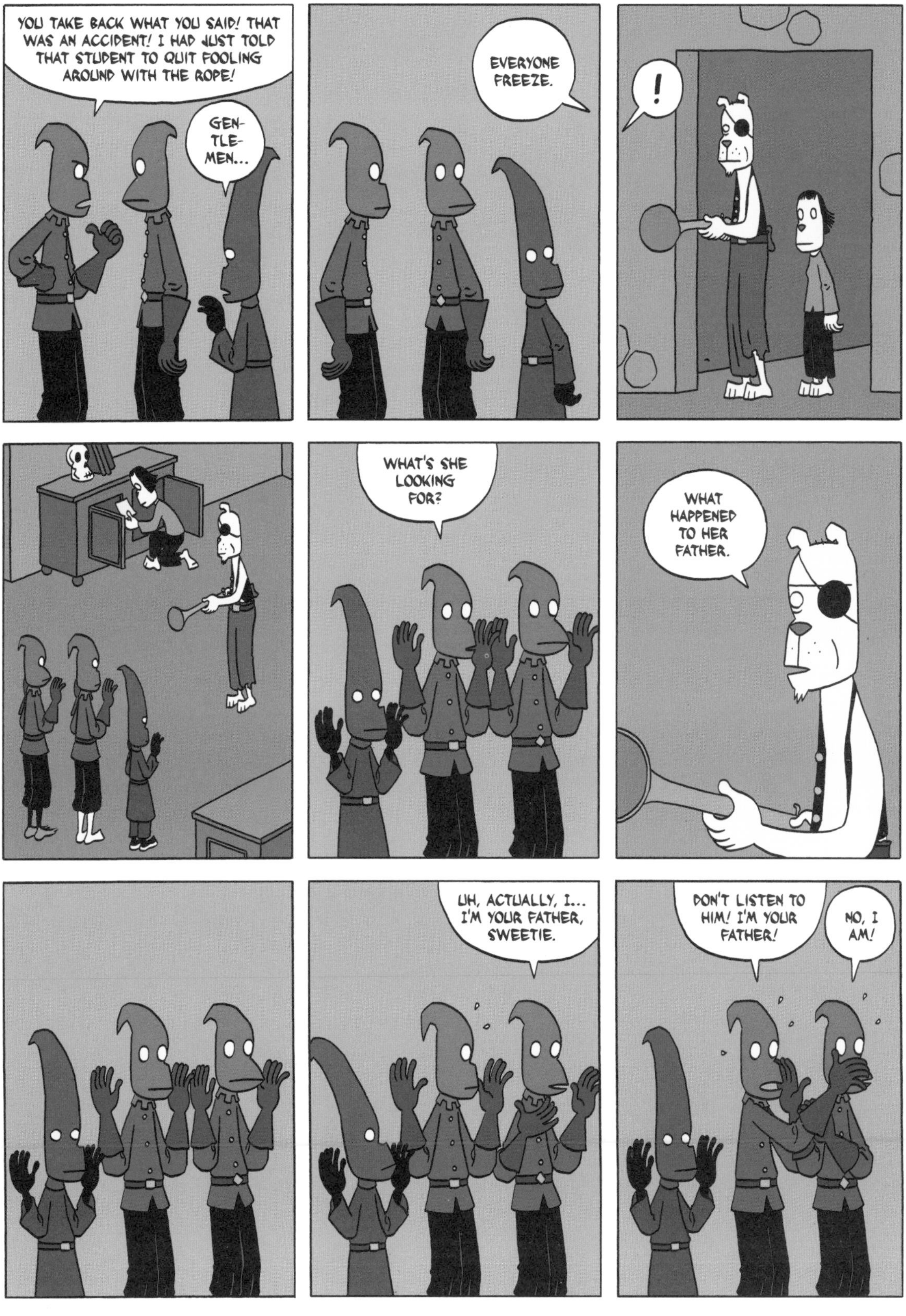
YOU TAKE BACK WHAT YOU SAID! THAT WAS AN ACCIDENT! I HAD JUST TOLD THAT STUDENT TO QUIT FOOLING AROUND WITH THE ROPE!
GEN-TLE-MEN...
EVERYONE FREEZE.
!
WHAT'S SHE LOOKING FOR?
WHAT HAPPENED TO HER FATHER.
UH, ACTUALLY, I... I'M YOUR FATHER, SWEETIE.
DON'T LISTEN TO HIM! I'M YOUR FATHER!
NO, I AM!

COME TO DADDY!
NO, HE'S NOT YOUR DADDY, I AM!
La Marie Galante
GIVE ME A HUG, PRINCESS!
NO, GIVE ME ONE!
SHUT ALL THOSE LIARS UP.
BLAM!
WE'RE DONE HERE.

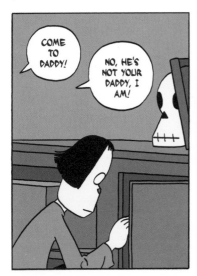

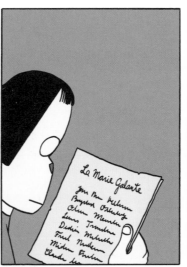

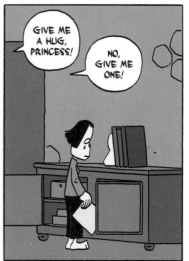

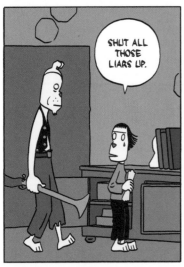

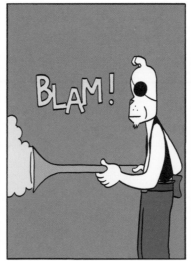

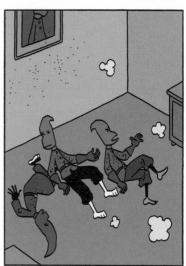

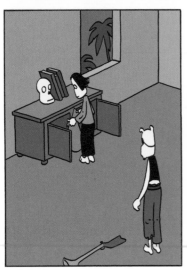

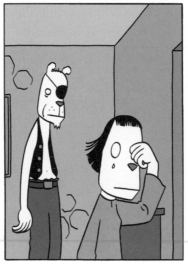

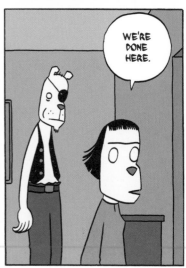

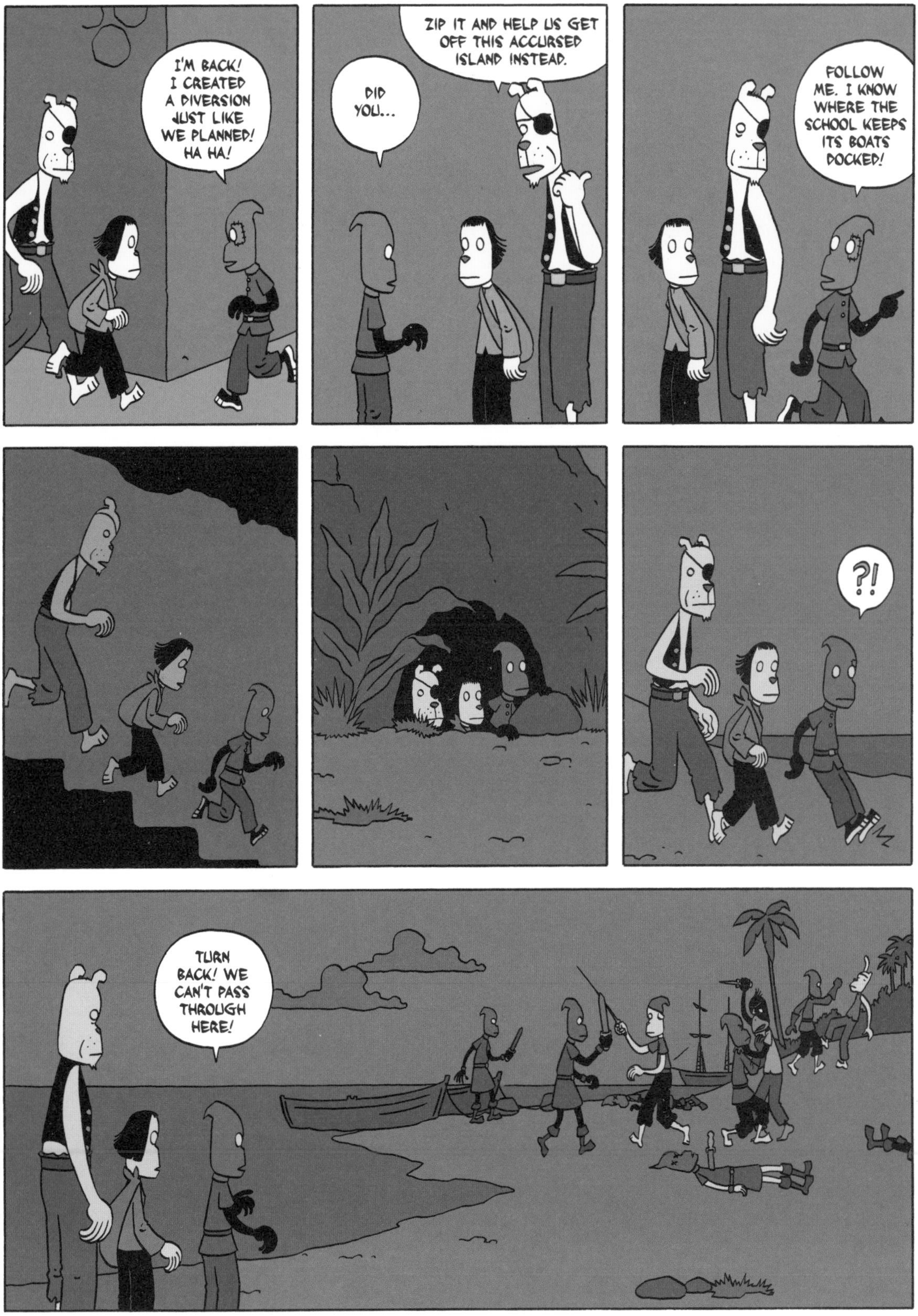
I'M BACK! I CREATED A DIVERSION JUST LIKE WE PLANNED! HA HA!
DID YOU...
ZIP IT AND HELP US GET OFF THIS ACCURSED ISLAND INSTEAD.
FOLLOW ME. I KNOW WHERE THE SCHOOL KEEPS ITS BOATS DOCKED!
?!
TURN BACK! WE CAN'T PASS THROUGH HERE!

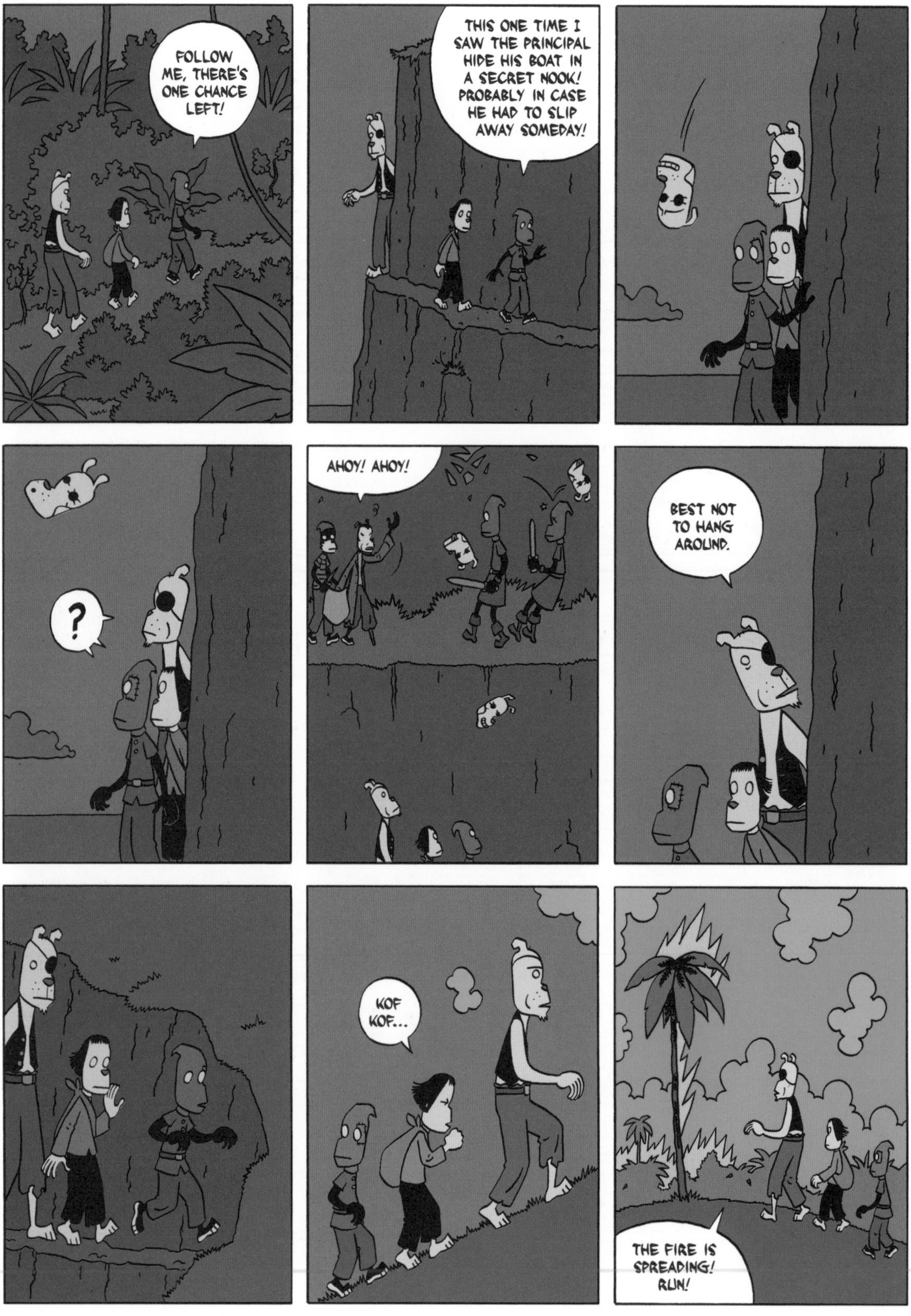
FOLLOW ME, THERE'S ONE CHANCE LEFT!
THIS ONE TIME I SAW THE PRINCIPAL HIDE HIS BOAT IN A SECRET NOOK! PROBABLY IN CASE HE HAD TO SLIP AWAY SOMEDAY!
?
AHOY! AHOY!
BEST NOT TO HANG AROUND.
KOF KOF...
THE FIRE IS SPREADING! RUN!

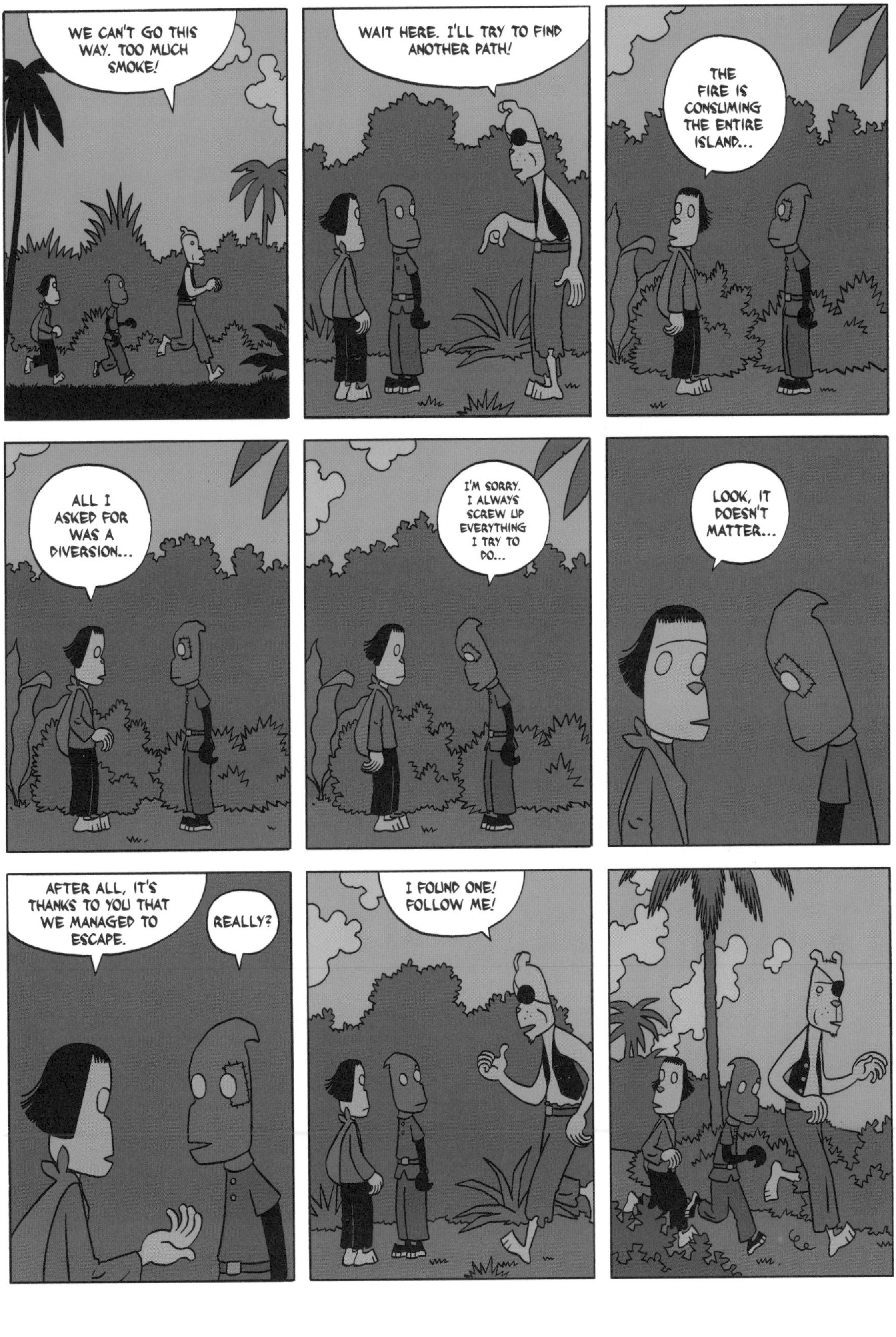
WE CAN'T GO THIS WAY. TOO MUCH SMOKE!
WAIT HERE. I'LL TRY TO FIND ANOTHER PATH!
THE FIRE IS CONSUMING THE ENTIRE ISLAND...
ALL I ASKED FOR WAS A DIVERSION...
I'M SORRY. I ALWAYS SCREW UP EVERYTHING I TRY TO DO...
LOOK, IT DOESN'T MATTER...
AFTER ALL, IT'S THANKS TO YOU THAT WE MANAGED TO ESCAPE.
REALLY?
I FOUND ONE! FOLLOW ME!

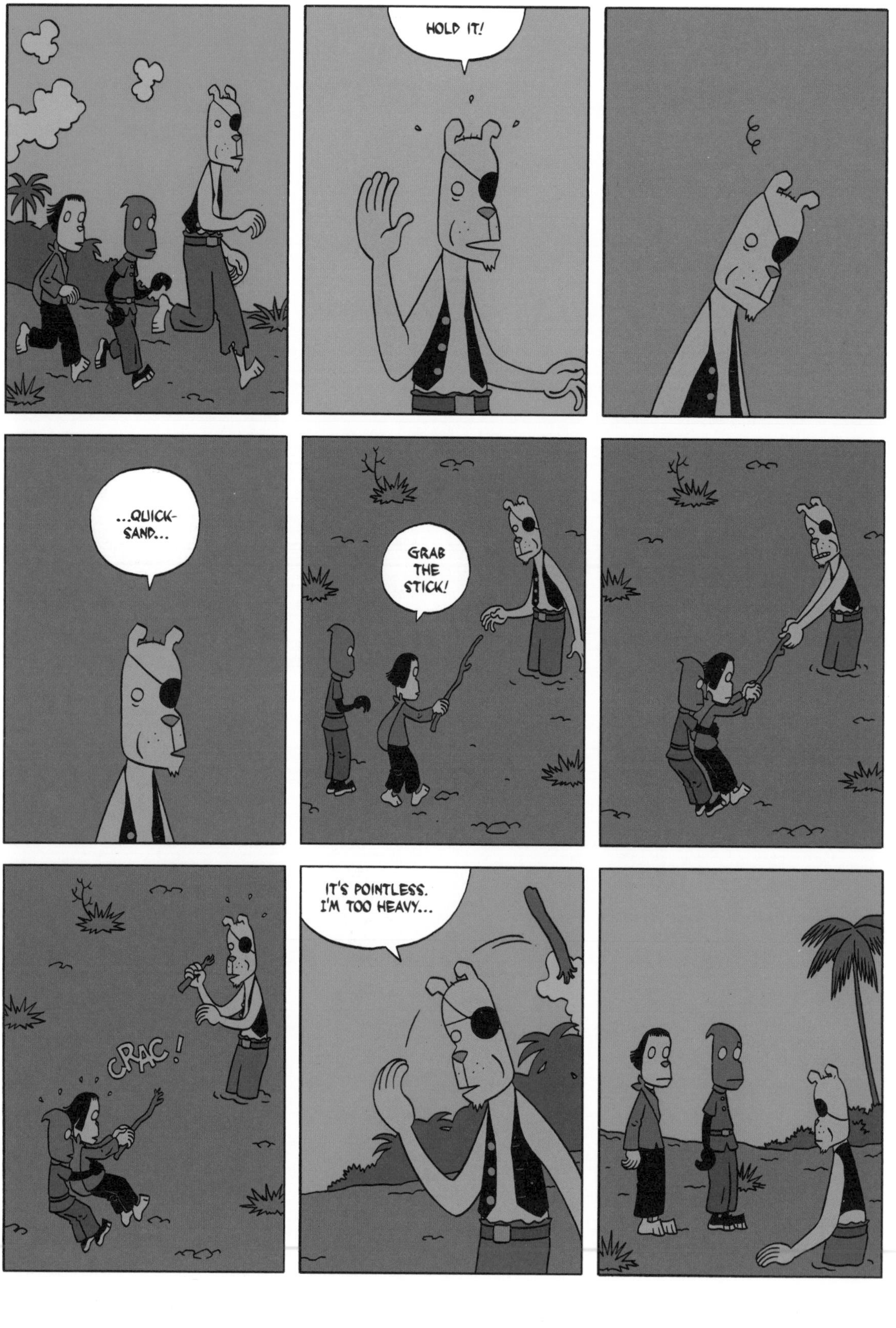
HOLD IT!
...QUICK-SAND...
GRAB THE STICK!
CRAC!
IT'S POINTLESS. I'M TOO HEAVY...

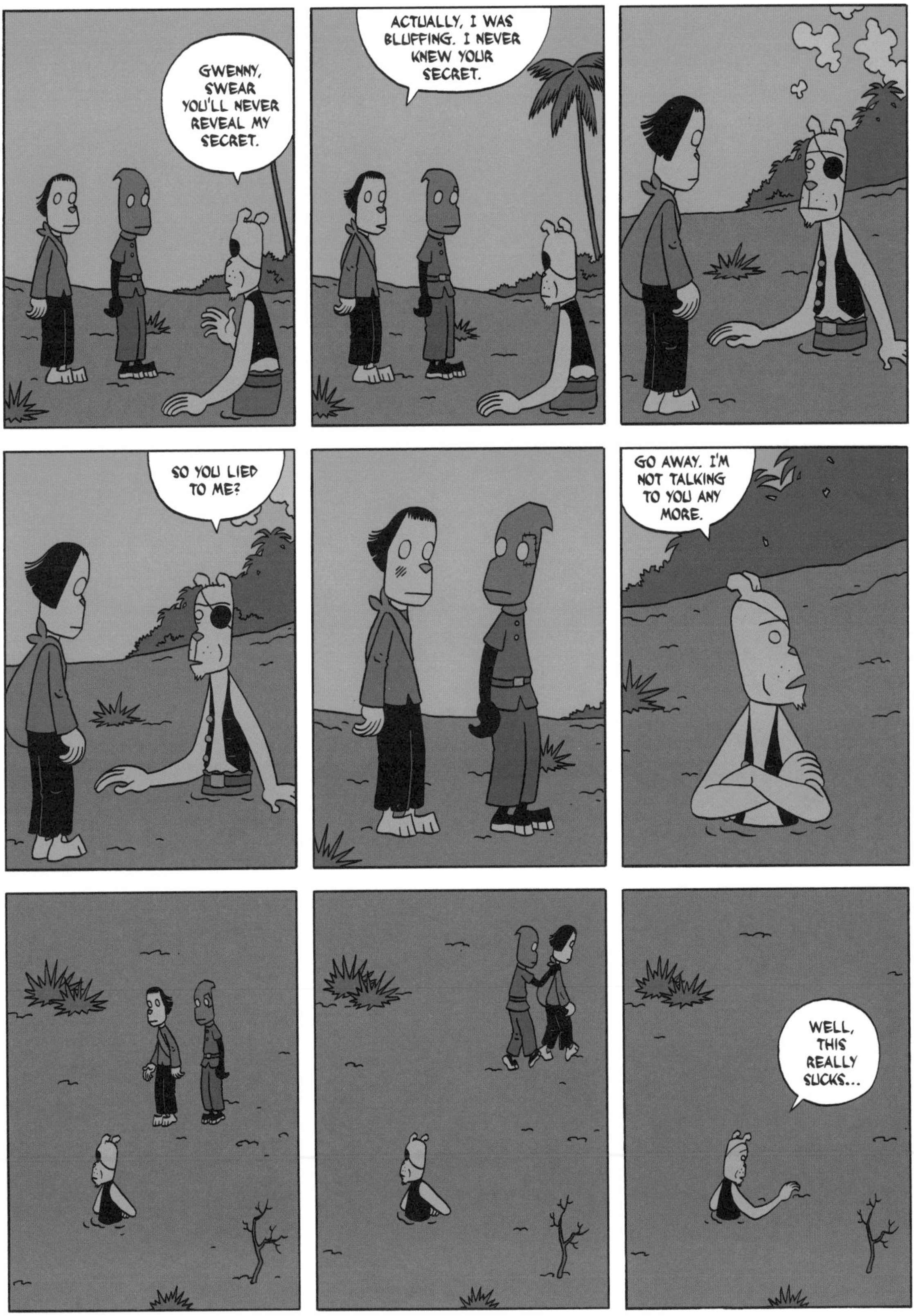
GWENNY, SWEAR YOU'LL NEVER REVEAL MY SECRET.
ACTUALLY, I WAS BLUFFING. I NEVER KNEW YOUR SECRET.
SO YOU LIED TO ME?
GO AWAY. I'M NOT TALKING TO YOU ANY MORE.
WELL, THIS REALLY SUCKS...

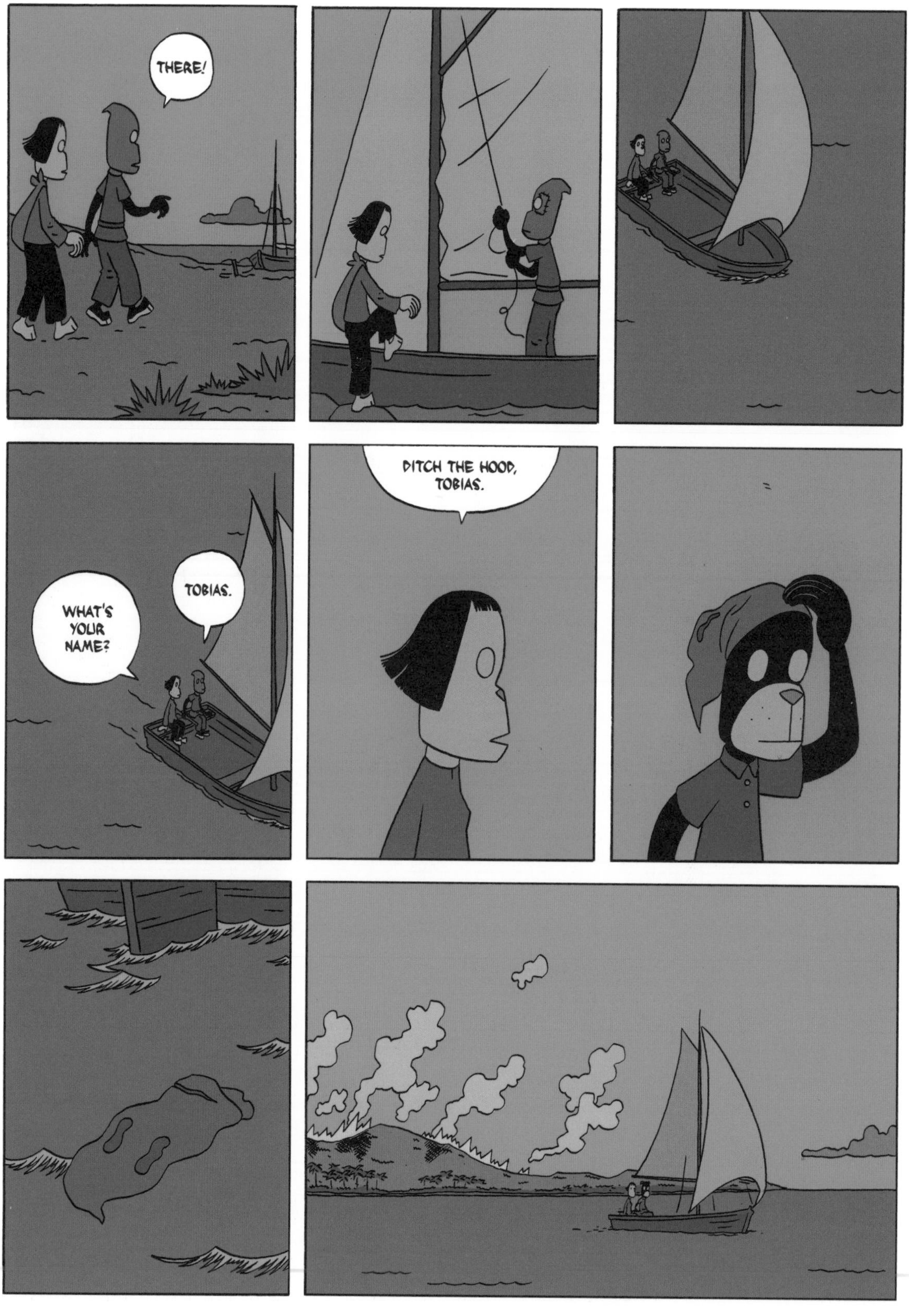
THERE!
WHAT'S YOUR NAME?
TOBIAS.
DITCH THE HOOD, TOBIAS.

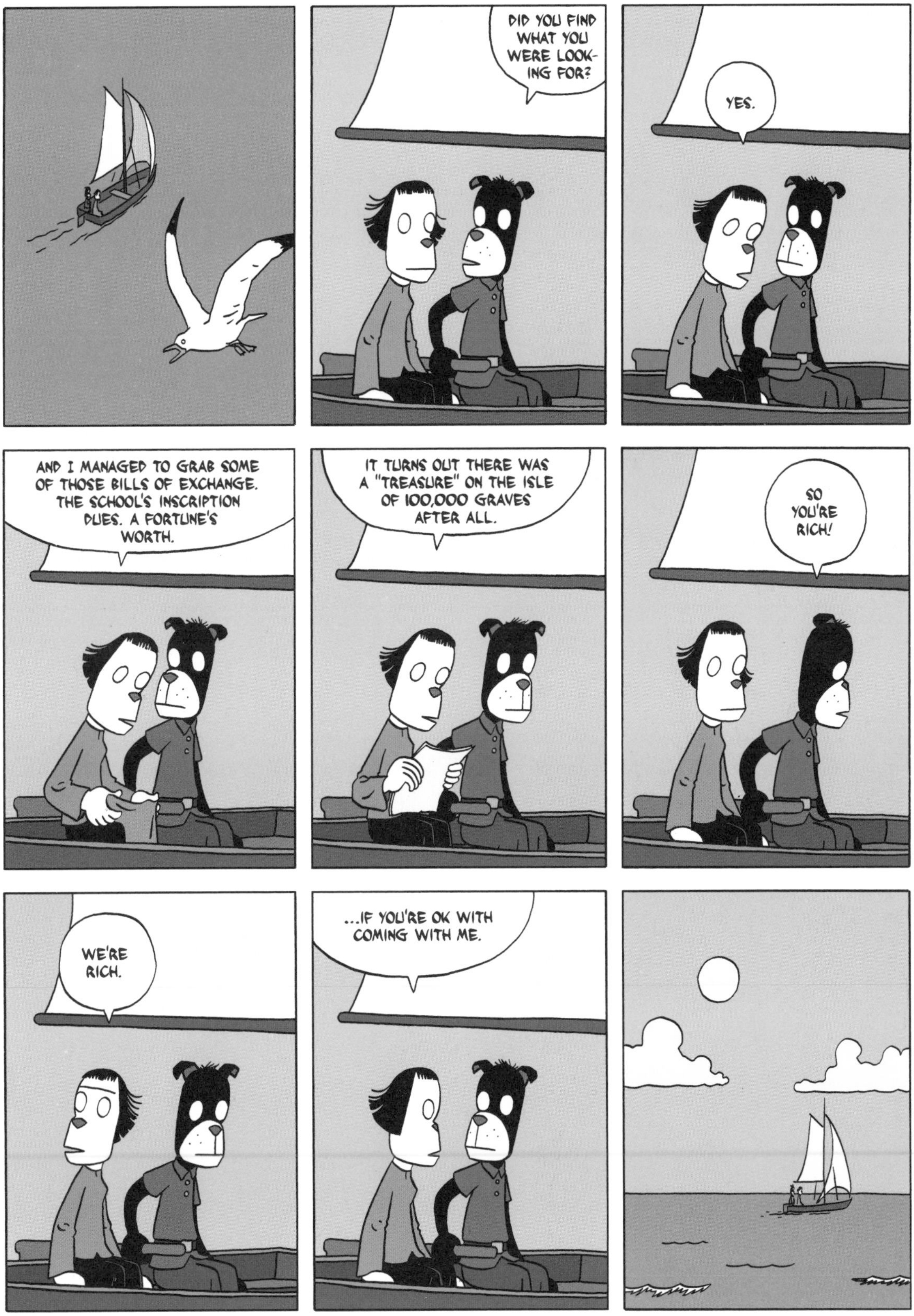
DID YOU FIND WHAT YOU WERE LOOKING FOR?
YES.
AND I MANAGED TO GRAB SOME OF THOSE BILLS OF EXCHANGE. THE SCHOOL'S INSCRIPTION DUES. A FORTUNE'S WORTH.
IT TURNS OUT THERE WAS A "TREASURE" ON THE ISLE OF 100,000 GRAVES AFTER ALL.
SO YOU'RE RICH!
WE'RE RICH.
...IF YOU'RE OK WITH COMING WITH ME.

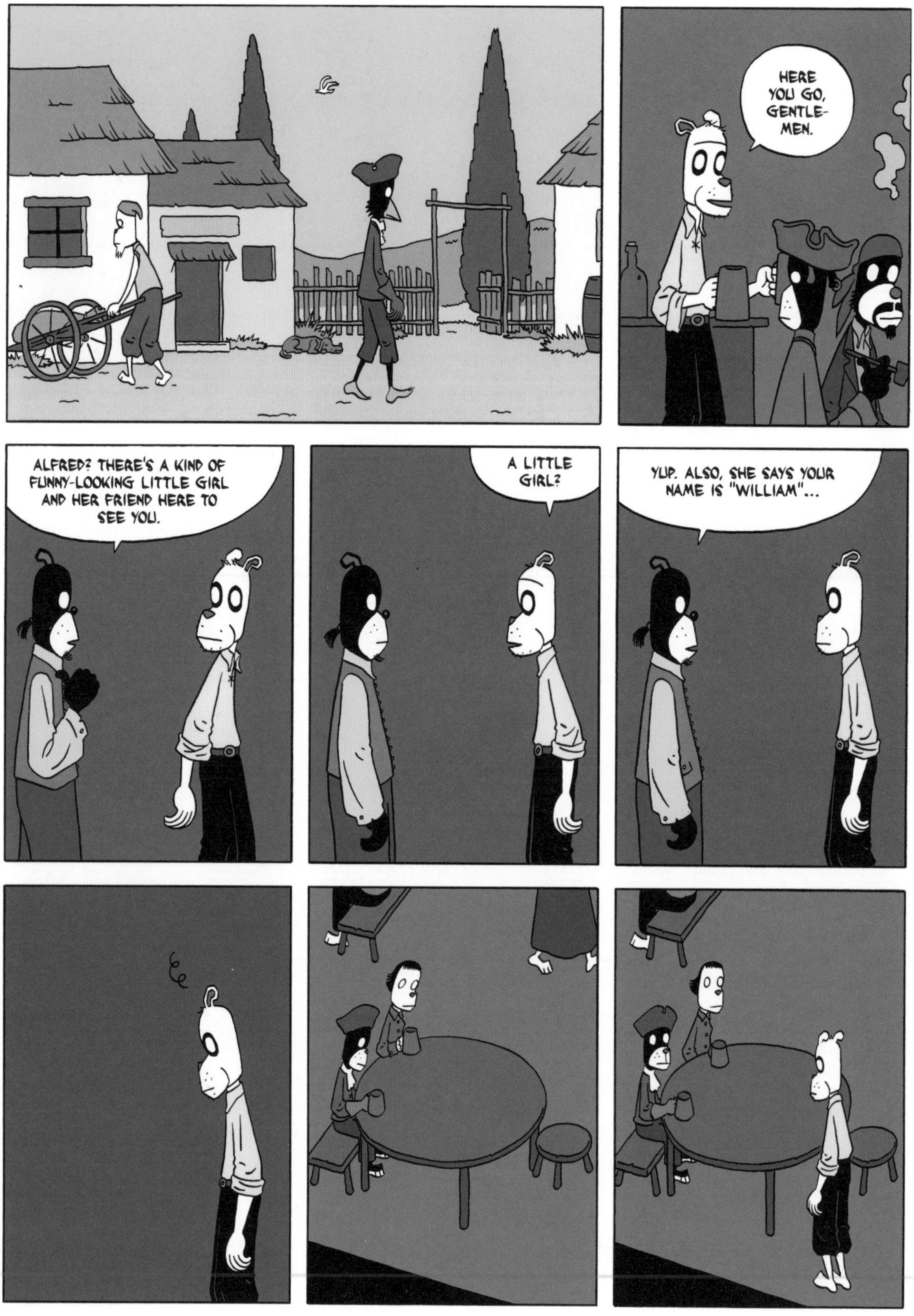
HERE YOU GO, GENTLE-MEN.
ALFRED? THERE'S A KIND OF FUNNY-LOOKING LITTLE GIRL AND HER FRIEND HERE TO SEE YOU.
A LITTLE GIRL?
YUP. ALSO, SHE SAYS YOUR NAME IS "WILLIAM"...

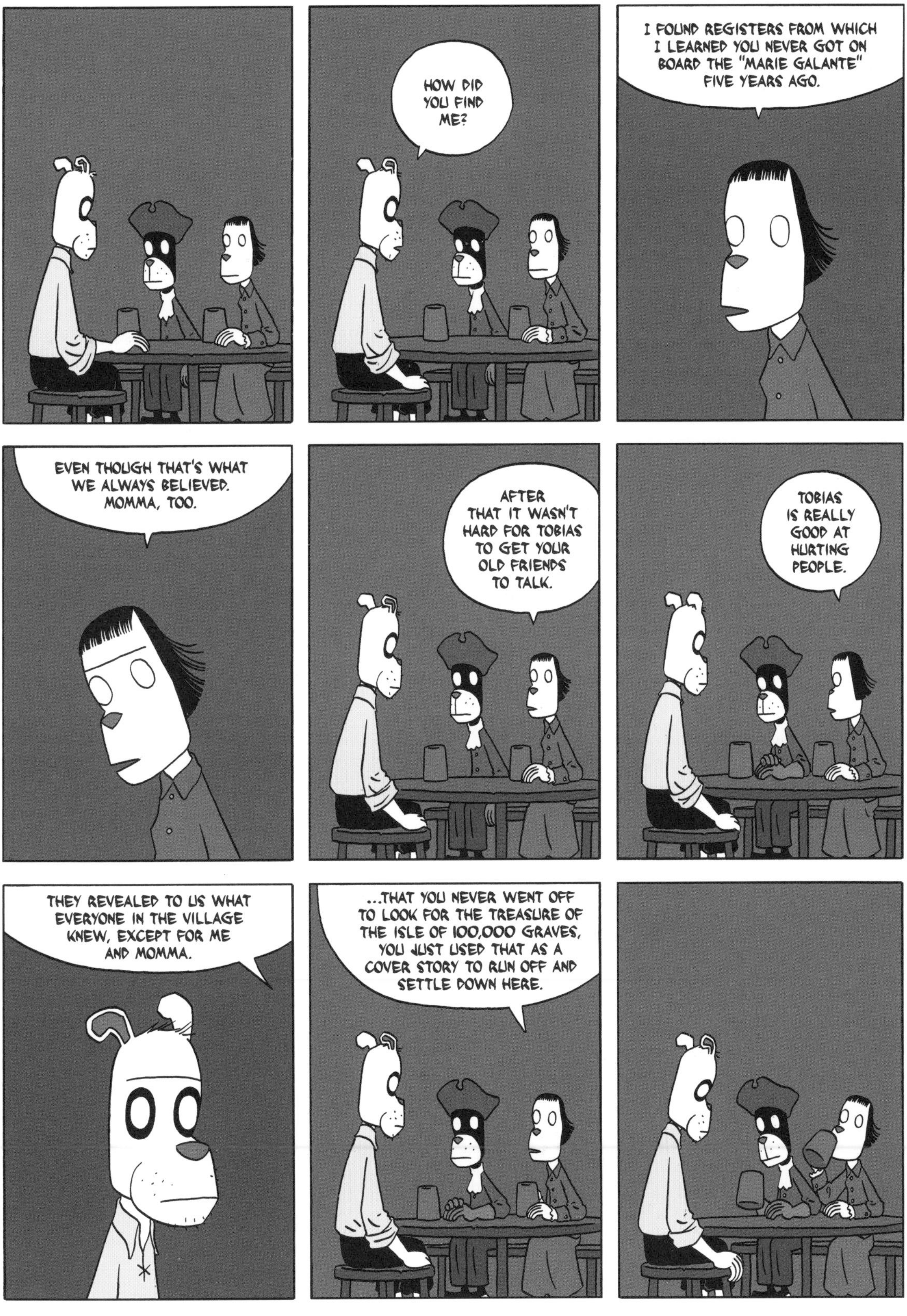
HOW DID YOU FIND ME?
I FOUND REGISTERS FROM WHICH I LEARNED YOU NEVER GOT ON BOARD THE "MARIE GALANTE" FIVE YEARS AGO.
EVEN THOUGH THAT'S WHAT WE ALWAYS BELIEVED. MOMMA, TOO.
AFTER THAT IT WASN'T HARD FOR TOBIAS TO GET YOUR OLD FRIENDS TO TALK.
TOBIAS IS REALLY GOOD AT HURTING PEOPLE.
THEY REVEALED TO US WHAT EVERYONE IN THE VILLAGE KNEW, EXCEPT FOR ME AND MOMMA.
...THAT YOU NEVER WENT OFF TO LOOK FOR THE TREASURE OF THE ISLE OF 100,000 GRAVES, YOU JUST USED THAT AS A COVER STORY TO RUN OFF AND SETTLE DOWN HERE.

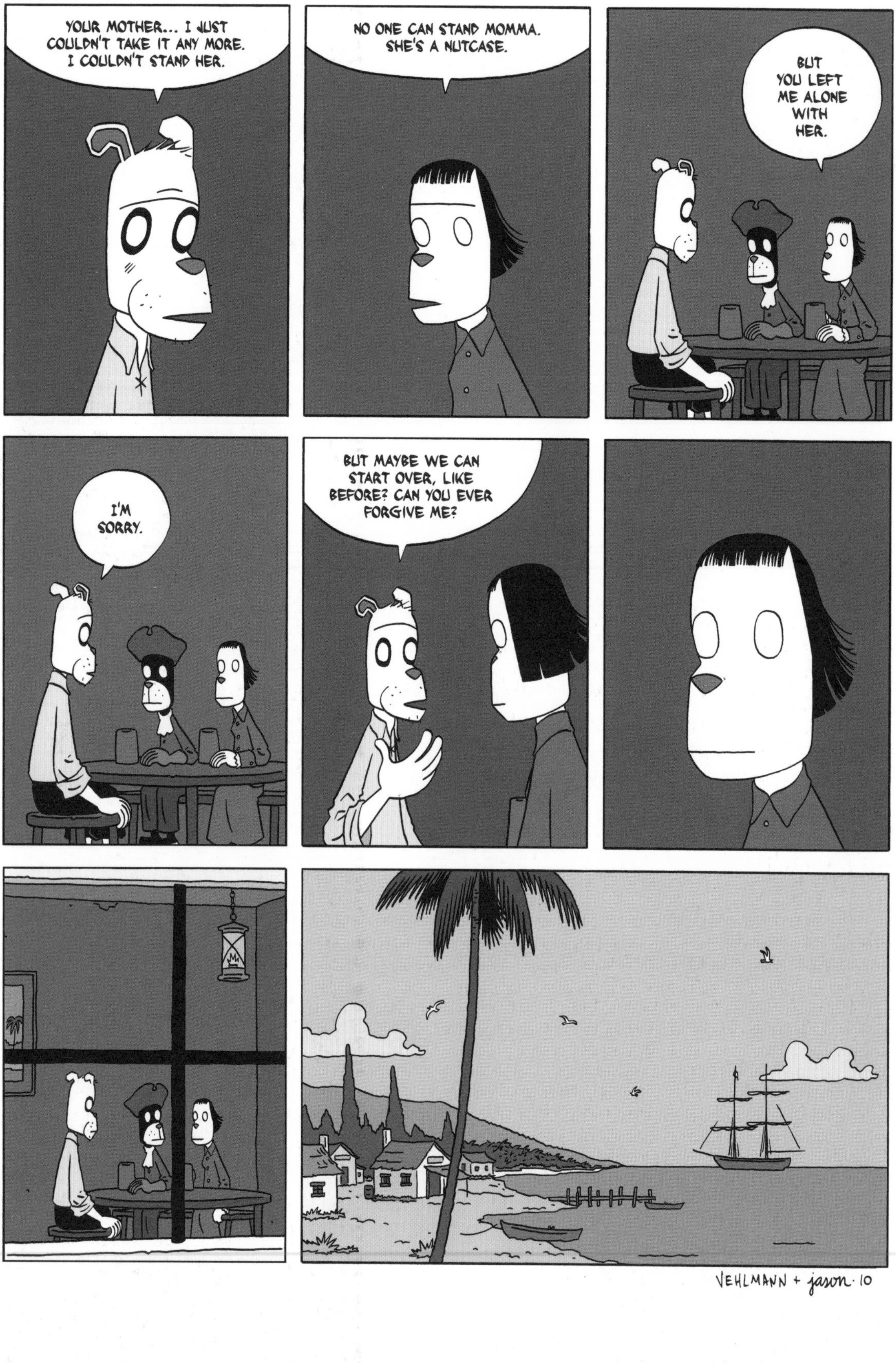
YOUR MOTHER... I JUST COULDN'T TAKE IT ANY MORE. I COULDN'T STAND HER.
NO ONE CAN STAND MOMMA. SHE'S A NUTCASE.
BUT YOU LEFT ME ALONE WITH HER.
I'M SORRY.
BUT MAYBE WE CAN START OVER, LIKE BEFORE? CAN YOU EVER FORGIVE ME?
VEHLMANN + jason · 10